Heather Angel's
COUNTRYSIDE

Heather Angel's
COUNTRYSIDE

written and photographed by
HEATHER ANGEL

[signature: Heather Angel]

MICHAEL JOSEPH/RAINBIRD
In association with
CHANNEL FOUR TELEVISION COMPANY LIMITED
and YORKSHIRE TELEVISION LIMITED

First published in Great Britain in 1983
by Michael Joseph Ltd
44 Bedford Square, London WC1 and
The Rainbird Publishing Group Ltd
40 Park Street, London W1Y 4DE
who designed and produced the book

ISBN 0 7181 2284 4

Editor: David Burnie
Design: Lee Griffiths
Production: Dee Maple
Indexer: Michele Clarke

Colour origination by Gilchrist Brothers Ltd, Leeds
Printed by William Collins, Sons & Company Ltd,
Glasgow

Half-Title: *A hedgerow silhouetted against the setting sun.*
Frontispiece: *Giant polypore and bracken on an old tree stump.*

ACKNOWLEDGMENTS
Heather Angel would like to thank everyone who so
willingly gave their time to answer many queries, to
suggest possible sites and to guide her round some
of them. After visiting over 50 locations, ease of
access for both television crews and the public
determined the selection of the final twenty. In
particular, the Yorkshire Naturalists' Trust, the
Lancashire Naturalists' Trust, the National Trust, the
Nature Conservancy Council, the Royal Society for
the Protection of Birds, Malham Tarn Field Centre,
the National Gardens Scheme, the Council for Places
to Worship, the Duchy of Lancaster Estate, the
Bolton Abbey Estate, and the staff in the
Scarborough Reference Library, were especially
helpful. Many individuals were also a tremendous
help, notably: Chris Baines, Dr Derrick Boatman, The
Rev Cuthbert Blackmore, Jim Bolton, Norma
Chapman, Giles Cooper, Mr H P Dobson, Mr C P
Evans, Mr & Mrs Philip Gilchrist, Mr P I Hall, John
Hampton, Colin Hawes, Debbie Holton, Philip
Horton, John Houston, Diane Hughes, Peter Jones,
Major Ian Kibble, Jack Lavin, Fred Leigh, Ian Massey,
Roger Mitchell, Brian Phillips, Graham Price, Richard
Price, Ivan Proctor, Mrs Philippa Rakusen, Philip
Rothwell, Dr Mark Seaward, Dr Phil Smith, Athol
Wallis, Stephen Warburton, Geoff Welch, Derek
Whitely, John Wilson, David Wright and Mrs Barbara
Yorke. In addition, Heather Angel would especially
like to thank Express Design Service for processing
her films so quickly; Julie Burchett, Mary Stafford
Smith and Kate West for their speedy typing; Jan
McLachlan and Helen Doncaster for their resourceful
researching; Dr Paul Whalley for checking the
butterfly chart; Graham Watts and Peter Cook from
Yorkshire Television for respectively producing and
researching my slots for the Channel 4 programme
Making the Most of . . . and Martin Angel for his
constant support and encouragement.

CONTENTS

A WOODLAND WAKES

Forge Valley Woods lie in the spectacular setting of a steep-sided gorge in the North Yorkshire Moors National Park. This gorge, which is up to 100 metres (330 feet) deep in some places, was carved out by the River Derwent when it was forced to follow a new course after its old route became blocked by glacial debris (see A *ribbon of life*).

The plants which first colonised the gorge would have been quite different from the ones in the woods today. Originally, when the climate was cooler, dwarf shrubs grew on the tundra-like terrain and it was only when the climate became warmer and wetter that forest trees and shrubs such as hazel, and later oak, elm and alder began to invade, providing food and shelter for many insects and birds.

It was the introduction of iron smelting that brought about permanent changes to the woodland. The valley forge probably originated in the thirteenth century, and would have been operated by Benedictine monks from Hackness Priory. Cinder hills and shallow pits marked on maps of the North Riding dales, compiled in the 1200s, are proof that primitive forges and furnaces were in existence even at that time, and there is little doubt that later in the century many abbeys and priories had forges working full blast. A 1798 print of the valley forge shows it set against a riverine woodland backcloth with a cascading waterfall, and among the buildings are a smelting-mill, a large water-wheel and a high chimney.

In springtime, wild garlic blooms carpet the ground in Forge Valley Woods.

Although the valley is several miles away from the nearest town, it was a suitable site for a forge because of the ready power supply (from the water of the River Derwent) and the plentiful oaks from which charcoal could be made. Nothing is now left of the forge itself, but its legacy is still visible in the woods. The remnants of old coppiced oaks are evidence that the trees were periodically felled at ground level to provide wood for charcoal, and among them are many of the imported sycamore trees which were planted in the valley to replace the slower-growing native trees that had been cut down.

It is not known for certain when the sycamore was first introduced to Britain, although Chaucer, writing in the fourteenth century, speaks of it as a rare exotic. Once it arrived it spread rapidly by means of its winged seeds which spin down from the trees like miniature helicopters. Sycamores are now a familiar feature of the British countryside, either as large solitary specimens growing in the open, or as more slender trees crowded in a woodland. Where they grow alone on dales and hillsides in the north, they enhance an otherwise treeless landscape, but when they invade a woodland they make it, from a naturalist's point of view, much less interesting. The large leaves open in spring and allow few chinks of light to penetrate down through the overhead canopy, which creates a shady woodland floor with a poor selection of wild flowers.

Wild garlic, or ramsons, is one of the few spring flowers which tolerates shade, and this grows in great profusion beneath the sycamores

A marsh tit with a beakful of caterpillars pauses before returning to its nest.

in Forge Valley. In May, huge drifts of white flowers stand out against the pointed green leaves. Wild garlic, which is closely related to the culinary garlic, onion and leek, can be instantly recognised by the pungent smell which permeates an entire woodland, and if its leaves are crushed underfoot, the damaged cells release an even stronger aroma.

In places where the air is clean, tar spot fungus often attacks sycamore leaves, producing several distinctive black spots on each leaf, but since this fungus will not tolerate air pollution, it rarely occurs on sycamores growing in an urban setting. Compared with the leaves of our native oak, those of the sycamore are poor food for insects. Only some 15 species feed on this tree – a mere fraction of the several

hundred which feed on oak leaves. In fact, more kinds of insects live associated with the oak tree than with any other tree (or plant) in Britain. This statistic is not merely of academic interest, for a wider variety of insects provides a wider range of potential food for birds, so that oak woodlands are particularly rich in wildlife.

It is certainly no accident that the breeding time of insect-eating woodland birds is closely synchronised with the spring boom in the insect population. Anyone who has observed parent birds feeding their fledglings will know that they work throughout the daylight hours bringing in caterpillars and other insects to satiate the gaping mouths of their hungry offspring.

To name but a few of the several thousand insect species which live on the oak tree, there are caterpillars and beetles which munch the leaves, predatory bugs which live beneath the bark and emerge to feed on passing prey, weevils which infest acorns, mosquitoes which live in rot-holes, and stag beetle larvae which spend five years developing in rotten stumps.

Among some of the insects which feed directly on the oak are more than fifty kinds of gall wasp which are responsible for a variety of abnormal growths on leaves or on twigs. These arise in response to the feeding of the wasp larvae which stimulates the oak tissues to swell around the developing insects and envelop them in a gall. Spongy oak apples are galls which originate from the oak buds in May, just as the oak leaves are opening. From a single oak apple, as many as several hundred wasps emerge. The custom of wearing an oak sprig with an oak apple on May 29th – Oak Apple Day – commemorates the Restoration of the Monarchy, when Charles II returned from exile to this country in 1660.

At first sight, it might seem unethical to fell any trees in what is now a National Nature Reserve, but successful conservation is rarely achieved by simply erecting a boundary fence;

vigorous species which would otherwise swamp surrounding plants have to be kept in check. Groups of sycamores are now being felled in Forge Valley to be replaced by the oak and ash trees which would occur in a native woodland, thereby encouraging a wider variety of plants and wildlife.

In spring, the contrast in the plants beneath the sycamores and beneath the mixture of oak, ash and hazel, is remarkable. Whereas the sycamore stands produce little more than wild garlic, under the mixed trees there is a succession of spring flowers for which British woods are famed, beginning with dog's mercury, followed by wood anemone, wood sorrel, primrose, bugle, bluebells and red campion.

We take bluebells very much for granted, for Britain is the focal point of the distribution of the wild hyacinth, or the pentacostal bells as they are also known, but if you cross the Channel, you will not find bluebells enhancing European woods, except in parts of France. Small wonder then, that European and American visitors to our land marvel at the intense blue carpets, which moved Tennyson to write that they 'seem like heaven breaking up through the earth'. Because we associate bluebells so much with wooded areas, it comes as something of a surprise to see them thriving among bracken on exposed ground on many seabird islands off our southwest coastline. Bluebells have suffered greatly in post-war years as more and more people have ready access to the countryside. It is not so much the picking of the flowers which harms the plants, as the trampling of the leaves underfoot, for it is the continued growth of the leaves after flowering which builds up the food reserves in the underground bulbs for the next year's blooms.

Man no longer gathers parts of woodland plants to cure his ailments, or as ready sources of useful substances, but in the past, both wild garlic and bluebells were utilised. Wild garlic was believed to draw moles from the ground and was generally regarded as a healer and an aphrodisiac. Measles were allegedly cured by wrapping nine separate pieces of linen each spread with powdered wild garlic from nine

One of the glories of a British woodland in spring is the haze of colour created by massed bluebells.

Where Forge Valley's lime-laden streams seep out of the hillside, deposits of hard tufa coat anything that lies in the water's path.

bulbs around an infected child. After the child was nursed for nine days, the linen was buried in the garden and the child would then be cured. (We now know that the duration of the illness is approximately nine days anyway!) The sap from bluebell leaves provided a gum which was used in the Middle Ages for fixing feathers to arrow shafts, while in Elizabethan times ruffs were stiffened from a starch obtained from bluebell bulbs.

Among the carpets of wild flowers in spring, clumps of mosses and ferns also grow, including the attractive hard fern which produces two different kinds of fronds or leaves. The broader evergreen sterile fronds grow out as a neat rosette, near the ground, and persist all year, whereas the erect fertile fronds which resemble a fish's backbone grow up from the centre of the rosette each summer, and die down in the winter. It is these fronds which produce the fern's spores.

Even in the height of summer, the slopes of Forge Valley Woods are remarkably damp, which is why there are raised duckboards on many parts of the public footpath, and why succulent plants such as golden saxifrage can thrive here. This persistent dampness originates from the numerous streams which burst out from the hillside as springs. Many of the springs issue from limestone and carry lime in solution so that when the water evaporates a limy deposit is left on any twig, leaf or shell lying in the stream-bed. As layer upon layer of lime builds up, a hard calcareous deposit, called tufa, develops which resembles solid rock but is considerably lighter because it is coarse and spongy. These tufa streams run down the hillside as brown ribbons coating all objects in their path.

An account of Forge Valley written in 1928 describes a petrifying spring as having stalactites hanging from the edge 'which might be big and strong if only the visitor would let them grow'. There is also a mention of a complete nest of a mistle-thrush – eggs and all – being placed beneath the falling waters of a tufa stream and left for 15 months. When it was removed it had 'turned completely to stone' and was sold for five shillings. A less destructive way of turning objects to 'stone' can be seen at Knaresborough's Dropping Well where there is always an array of old socks and boots strung up beneath the dripping water in various stages of petrification.

A woodland in spring, just before the leaf canopy has completely filled out, can make one of the most fascinating walks for anyone with their senses alert. Keen eyes will spot animal tracks – especially deer slots – on damp ground. There will be a constant chorus of bird song, interrupted perhaps by the sharp tapping of a woodpecker, and, if there is an infestation of caterpillars, the munching of millions of tiny jaws into the overhead leaves and the continual 'rain' of their droppings onto the floor. A deciduous woodland is so much more than a collection of trees.

THE WORLD OF A POND

Centuries ago, the pond was the focal point of village life. It provided water for the villagers, their farm animals, and was also a welcome watering stop for heavy horses pulling loaded wagons before they went on their journey. So important was a pond to a rural community, that villages often grew up around the site of an existing pond, and if one was not already in existence, a pond would be dug, preferably on the site of a natural spring. Alternatively, a pond was created by damming a stream. During the peak of the Enclosure Acts, when the vast open fields were being carved up into smaller units bounded by hedgerows, many ponds had to be created so that farm animals had somewhere to drink. Dew ponds were a special feature of chalk downland in southern England. Each pond was sited in a natural shallow basin which was fed by rain water running off the surrounding hills. After the dew pond was dug out, the bottom was waterproofed by lining it with alternating layers of clay and straw, and finished off with a layer of flints. The name dew pond arose from the misguided belief that the ponds were filled only with dew. Now, most of these hollows have become completely grassed over and only a few dew ponds still hold water.

Ponds were not only used to supply drinking water: some sported a ducking stool, on which petty thieves were plunged into the water for their misdemeanours. Even when traction engines began to supersede draught horses as a means of pulling wagons and farm machinery, they were still topped up with pond water so they could generate the steam power. At one time, ponds were also plentiful on farms where they provided drinking water for stock, but most have now been replaced with water troughs fed by piped water. Mill ponds, fish ponds and duck decoys, each designed for a specific use, also harboured a rich assortment of plants and aquatic life. Monasteries always had their stew ponds where the monks kept carp, so they had a ready supply of fish to eat on Fridays, when the consumption of meat was forbidden.

During this century, many ponds have fallen into disrepair. When they are no longer managed by periodic cleaning out, and when their banks are not trampled by cattle and horses coming to drink, plants soon move in, ultimately filling the entire pond, creating first a marsh and then scrub which may finally give way to trees. All too often, neglected ponds have been used as dumping grounds for old cars and other eyesores, while others have been filled in to provide building land.

In a picturesque village setting in Yorkshire lies a pair of ponds bisected by a sloping brickwork structure known as the 'lush'. When the level of the water in the top pond rises, it spills over the lush and down the slope like a miniature weir into the lower pond. During the drier months, the water flow is restricted to a narrow open channel which runs all the way along the top of the lush to be discharged into the lower pond through a broad central outflow. The fast current in the open channel provides ideal conditions for willow moss to grow without having to compete with other aquatic

The peaceful scene of a village pond belies the struggle for existence beneath the water's surface.

Almost as if in a primaeval swamp, upright marestail spikes grow through a mat of floating algae.

plants. This is Britain's largest moss and the only truly aquatic one – a plant once used in Lapland for filling the spaces in house walls to exclude air and prevent fire.

There appears to be no recorded history of when these ponds were built, although they used to belong to a family who had lived in the area for 500 years.

A millstone was found in the garden of a house built beside the lower pond, which suggests that this was the site of two mills mentioned in the Domesday Book. If so, it would indicate that there was a pond there as early as the eleventh century. It is also rumoured that the church door was hidden in the pond prior to Cromwell's visit to the area in the seventeenth century. Current local opinion,

however, seems to favour the view that the existing ponds may have been made when the adjacent pasture was enclosed in 1780.

The ponds are fed by a beck which originates from an underground spring, so that even in the height of summer it gushes out icy-cold water. The aquatic plant which dominates the ponds is the marestail, which is a flowering plant and therefore no relation of the primitive non-flowering horsetails which it somewhat resembles. Its common name arose from the old mistaken belief that it was a female plant of the horsetail, hence mare's tail. By winter, the stems flop into the water and begin to decay, but in spring, new stems, with their fine leaves arranged in whorls, emerge above the water. The inconspicuous greenish flowers which arise at the junction of the leaves and stem are wind-pollinated.

When I first visited the ponds at the end of May, the marestail spikes were emerging and several pairs of coots had uprooted stems to build their nest mounds. Coots are adaptable birds, making use of whatever plants or objects are to hand to build their nests. In urban settings they improvise with plastic bags, and I once found a coot's nest on top of a discarded milk crate! Unlike grebes which build their nests on a floating platform, coot nests are firmly anchored to underwater plants, so that they run the risk of being submerged by floods. However, if necessary, they are able to build up their nests by as much as 10–20 centimetres (4–8 inches) in a matter of a few hours, even when the nest contains eggs, because nesting material is packed in beneath the eggs as the water level rises. Coots lay 4–8 mottled eggs and may rear two or more broods each year. When the young first hatch, they are fed by their parents, but they begin to fend for themselves once they are a week old. The chicks are particularly vulnerable to herons or to a pike lurking in the reeds underwater. Adult coots are easily recognisable by the white shield on the front of their heads and can often be seen tweaking off tips of emergent plants using the sharp cutting edges on their bills. They can also dive down to feed on submerged plants, using their elaborately lobed feet to propel them through the water, but they never remain underwater for more than a few seconds at a time. They also feed on nymphs of invertebrates, newts, small fish and occasionally on other birds' eggs and chicks.

During the breeding season, a coot spends much time defending its territory, striking an aggressive pose by lowering its head and raising its wings as it paddles furiously towards the intruder uttering a piercing call.

Young waterfowl lead a dangerous life, and adult moorhens, mallards and little grebes which also nest on ponds have difficulty in protecting their energetic fledglings. Female mallards know that both carrion crows and rats are quick to take advantage of careless offspring, and so they keep a wary eye on any youngster which breaks away from the brood.

Every year in spring frogs and toads make their way to ponds for spawning. Frogs are the first to return, the precise timing of their visit depending on the air temperature. Frogs in the warmer southwest corner of Britain breed several weeks before frogs in the northern part of the country. Data collected from a nationwide Frog Watch Survey made in 1981 enabled a frog spawn map to be compiled which clearly revealed the way in which spring moves up through Britain. In this year, frog spawn was found in Cornwall and the southern tip of Wales before February 11th, whereas in northern England and south Scotland, it was not found until after March 12th.

Toads generally breed later than frogs, although in years when spring comes late, they may overlap. Males begin to arrive before the females, and they attract a mate by croaking.

The combined noise of hundreds of croaking frogs or toads is often the best way of locating a breeding site. As frogs and toads migrate to their ancestral ponds, they often have to cross roads and then large numbers may be flattened, unless special precautions are taken. In some areas, warning signs plead for motorists to take care and local naturalists often assist by carrying frogs and toads safely across the road. Europeans seem to be more concerned about the welfare of their amphibians than we are in Britain, for toad tunnels have been built beneath autobahns in Germany and main roads may even be closed for a few days during the peak of the migration.

As soon as a male frog or toad meets up with a female, he climbs onto her back, using his forelegs to grasp her belly. When the female lays her eggs into the water, the male fertilises them before the jelly layer around the eggs takes up water and swells. Frogs lay their spawn in clumps which sink at first, then rise up to the surface, whereas toads lay egg ropes which become entwined around underwater plants.

Dead leaves are just one of many natural materials used by coots in building nest mounds.

Just before tadpoles hatch, they resemble little black commas, but within a few days a distinct head and a muscular tail forms and later the legs develop. Although each female frog lays 2,000 – 4,000 eggs, the large numbers are very necessary since they are preyed upon by fish and water birds as well as the larvae and adults of the predatory diving beetle, and most of them do not survive past the tadpole stage.

Many small invertebrates live year-round in ponds, including flatworms which creep over the underside of stones on a mat of microscopic hairs, freshwater shrimps, water boatmen and snails. Even in winter, when the surface of a pond has iced over, these animals can still be found alive in the unfrozen water beneath the icy covering, often burrowing into the muddy bottom. As the floating and marginal plants die back at the onset of winter, their remains fall down to the bottom of the pond, where they provide a useful source of food during the winter. When the water temperature drops, freshwater organisms are less active and so they utilise much less oxygen and energy than when they are actively searching for food and a mate during the warmer months. Mayflies, caddis-flies and dragonflies emerge from ponds as adult insects after spending many months of their lives as aquatic larvae. The beauty of a dragonfly belies its true predatory nature – both as an adult and as a larva. Dragonflies are equipped with a huge pair of compound eyes which are essential for tracking down the prey. The fast-flying adults capture their prey while in flight, and alight to consume it. The larva adopts a much more leisurely, but no less cunning, technique for catching its prey, which may be tadpoles, the larvae of many other insects and even fish. Inching its way forward

For a brief few days each spring, frogs instinctively make their way to shallow water to mate and lay spawn in their ancestral breeding sites.

towards the unsuspecting prey, the larva suddenly attacks by shooting out a pair of strong, curving claws on the end of a highly extensible 'mask', which neatly folds away beneath the head when it is not in use. Once captured, the prey is brought up to the mouth where it is slowly eaten.

In the summer, swallows and house martins sweep in low over ponds to drink, and if there is an exposed muddy margin they can be seen scooping up mud for their mud nests. All day long, they twist and turn back and forth feeding on aerial insects, the swallows feeding much closer to the water than house martins or swifts.

The three-spined stickleback is probably the fish most commonly found in ponds. It is famous for its elaborate courtship display, which can be observed in an aquarium. In the spring, the male builds an underwater nest tunnel from pieces of algae and weeds, sticking them together by a secretion from his kidneys. By the time this is complete, he is sporting his colourful breeding dress, with a red throat and belly and blue eyes. He entices a drab-coloured female towards his nest by performing a zig-zag dance, and after she has entered the nest and spawned, he fertilises the eggs and stands guard over them until they hatch. He continues to protect the young fish by taking them into his mouth when danger threatens.

When ponds are stocked with trout for fishing, areas of open water free of water weeds have to be maintained so that cast hooks do not get snared among the weeds. In shallow water, where men can safely wade through weed beds, plants are removed either by cutting with long scythes or by dragging them from the bed with a rope. Once uprooted, the weeds float up to the surface, where they are dragged out and dumped on to the nearest bank. The removal of weeds destroys a source of food and shelter for a myriad of freshwater life.

As anyone who has dug their own garden pond will know, when a new water body is created, many aquatic organisms arrive unaided. Such opportunists include algae, duckweed, water fleas, snails, water beetles and the least welcome of all, mosquitoes. Algal spores and wind-borne seeds of plants will arrive quite by chance as winds blow them from one pond to another. Eggs of snails and sticky seeds of waterside plants may get carried on the feet of ducks or other water birds, while water beetles can fly in. Dragonflies and mayflies will take advantage of a new area of clean water for laying their eggs. The sudden appearance of duckweed carpeting the surface of a pond can originate from a tiny portion adhering to ducks' feet as they walk or fly from one pond to another. Once there, the duckweed rapidly buds off new plants. But birds are not the sole natural importer, for I have seen a toad clambering out of a canal along a towpath, with several tiny plants on its back. When larger aquatic plants are transplanted from one pond to another, it is more than likely that duckweed accidentally arrives with them.

It is heartening to know that village and farmyard ponds are no longer declining so rapidly and well over a thousand ponds have now been restored since the Save the Village Pond Campaign was launched in 1974. Garden ponds are on the increase and they provide useful – albeit small – breeding sites for amphibians and other aquatic life, so it looks as though ponds are in no immediate danger of completely disappearing from the British lowland landscape.

The showy flowers of yellow flags provide a striking contrast with the dense clumps of their green leaves.

A SCULPTURED LANDSCAPE

Anyone who sets eyes on a bare limestone landscape or pavement for the first time could be forgiven for thinking they have stumbled across a man-made set for a science fiction movie, for the grey, sometimes almost white, rock is so exquisitely sculptured. Yet all the shapes, which would delight any artist's eye, have been created entirely by natural means.

Except for small areas in Scotland and Wales, limestone pavements are confined to the north of England (the Yorkshire Pennines, Cumbria and the Morecambe Bay area in Lancashire) and the Burren on the west coast of Ireland in County Clare. The limestone from which the pavements are composed was formed beneath the sea from the accumulation of shells or the remains of skeletons of marine organisms, including corals. When the sea level dropped, these limestone beds became part of the land mass. Where ice sheets spread over the exposed rock, the combination of the weight and grinding action of millions of tons of ice slowly advancing over the surface gradually wore it down, and boulders and stones carried in the ice sheets acted like over-sized sandpaper, smoothing the rough surfaces. When the ice melted, some of the boulders and stones were left stranded on top of the pavement, where they can still be seen today in places like Norber near Austwick, where huge boulders made of Silurian rock perch incongruously on top of the limestone pavement.

After the last Ice Age the pavements began to be etched away, a process which has continued ever since. Compared with most rocks, limestone is relatively soft and can be dissolved by the action of acids. Pressure from the ice sheets left cracks which criss-crossed the surface, and these were gradually enlarged by the acids from plants growing over the limestone, as well as by acid rain. Even when the pavements were covered with a layer of glacial drift, (the material left behind after the retreat of glaciers), they were slowly being sculptured by the action of acids from overlying peat-forming plants.

When rain water falls it unites with carbon dioxide from the air, forming a weak acid. The acid rain water gradually dissolves away the limestone, enlarging the cracks until they become deep channels or 'grikes' surrounding the separate paving stones or 'clints'. Most grikes are narrow enough to step across quite easily, and usually only a metre or two (3 to 6 feet) deep, but some are as much as 6 metres (20 feet) in depth, so it is not surprising that from time to time an occasional sheep disappears as it loses its footing.

Running over the surface of the clints are shallow drainage channels, or gutters, known as runnels which carry the rain water into the grikes. It is the shape of these runnels, of small saucer-like pools, and of the smaller grikes which provide such fascinating sculptures, no two of which are repeated. On sloping pavements the runnels run in the direction of the slope, whereas on level pavements they form random patterns.

No sooner does it rain than the water drains away down through the runnels and the grikes

In a limestone pavement grike, a sycamore, distorted by wind and browsing sheep, struggles to survive.

Each spring, hart's tongue ferns emerge above damp limestone fissures as their new fronds unfurl.

into underground streams, which feed subterranean rivers only a few metres below the surface. If you are lucky and can find the path of a stream you will be able to hear the water beneath you if you put your ear to the ground.

The surface of the limestone pavement is not always as safe as it appears because some rocks are unattached at their base. More than once as I have walked over pavements, when I stepped on a clint it has suddenly tilted as it pivoted on a smaller rock beneath. But even this rocky landscape is threatened by man, for these water-worn rocks are much prized as rockery stones. Originally clints were laboriously levered out of place by means of crow-bars —

some of which remain projecting as rusty statues – but now tractors can make light work of removing natural pavements. Once destroyed, these unique habitats are lost forever, for it would require another Ice Age to smooth out the limestone surface yet again.

Part of the fun of walking over a pavement area is that, unlike a flowering meadow where all the plants grow out in the open, the slit-like shady grikes reveal their plants only when you are so close you can look straight down them. In these miniature canyons plants can thrive out of reach of browsing sheep in a hidden world below the surface rock. No matter how many times you may have walked over a single pavement, you may still come across a new and unexpected find, whether it be a flower, a fern or perhaps a moss.

Ferns and mosses both flourish in damp shady sites. The long strap-shaped leaves or fronds of the hart's tongue fern make it instantly recognisable. In the summer, brown lines develop on the underside of the fronds, each line containing clusters of spore-sacs which release their microscopic spores into the air and some of them are blown into soil pockets in other grikes. Often sharing the chimney-like home with the hart's tongue ferns are flowers such as dog's mercury, herb Robert, sanicle, wood anemone, wood sorrel and wild garlic, all shade-loving plants typical of woodland floors which thrive equally well in the damp grikes.

The flowers of the bloody cranesbill, a local but not uncommon plant, are a sure indication of a limestone or chalk terrain.

Where rain water collects in small surface pools, it traps just enough plant debris to form a humus in which seeds can germinate. Providing the area is not grazed by sheep, plants can then grow on top of the pavement – wild lily-of-the-valley with its exquisite-smelling white bell-shaped flowers and leaves which rustle in the wind, the eye-catching bright crimson blooms of the bloody cranesbill and the globe flower's distinctive yellow heads.

Although shrubs and even trees will grow on exposed pavements few bear much similarity to their counterparts elsewhere. Next time you are battling to stay upright against a head-on wind try crouching, or better still lying prone, and feel the difference. Shrubs which are constantly buffeted and pruned by wind end up growing flush with the ground. Both juniper and yew

creep over windy pavements forming dense mats – I have seen lop-sided bonsai-sized hawthorns no more than 50 centimetres (20 inches) high struggling to grow against the elements in the Burren. Here the only 'forests' are stunted 1-metre (3-foot) high hazel thickets.

Extensive limestone pavements lie around Ingleborough Peak, whose distinctive flat-topped profile is renowned by walkers, climbers, pot-holers and botanists. If you are prepared to climb to the 715-metre (2,345-foot) high summit you may be rewarded by a spectacular view, providing it is not shrouded by low cloud. The 6-hectare (15-acre) plateau is surrounded by a stone wall nearly one kilometre (half-a-mile) long which encloses an Iron Age hill fort, including the remains of 19 hut circles. The peak itself is capped by millstone grit, a kind of hard sandstone rock containing silica, and beneath this are shale, sandstone and limestone beds. But it is the Carboniferous limestone plateau lying between 335 and 440 metres (1,100 and 1,440 feet) high which has given rise to the spectacular scenery and such an interesting assemblage of plants that several nature reserves have been declared on Ingleborough's flanks. Here, quite respectable sycamore and ash trees have been allowed to grow up beyond the browsing limit of sheep. The shade cast by the branches of even a single tree creates a more humid microclimate beneath it allowing a mossy growth to establish itself in clear contrast to the surrounding unshaded rock.

There are even a few remnants of ash woods growing on these pavements, encouraging a very rich growth of plants in the grikes and on the clints of the shady floor. Ash trees produce winged seeds or keys which persist on the tree long after the leaves have fallen, and are a useful food source for birds during hard times. Each key is slightly twisted which causes it to spin as it falls thereby delaying the time it takes to reach the ground and increasing the likeli-

hood of it being dispersed away from the parent tree. Sycamore also has winged seeds and like those of ash; if they drop into a grike, they can germinate into saplings, but once they appear above the rock's surface, only a few survive persistent nibbling by rabbits or sheep to mature into trees.

Ingleborough's rock-strewn slopes are riddled with caves and potholes, a typical feature of limestone country. The warm periods in between the Ice Ages produced great volumes of glacial meltwater which accelerated the erosion and enlargement of the cave systems. Today, as water runs off the surface pavement down the grikes to seek out underground drainage channels, the caves are still growing. Gaping Ghyll beneath Ingleborough is the largest limestone cave in Britain. Its 104-metre (340-foot) deep shaft was first explored by a Frenchman, Martel, who took 23 minutes to reach its floor with the aid of a rope ladder. Now it is possible on two days each year to descend in a motorized bosun's chair in just 20 seconds flat! About 15 kilometres (9 miles) to the southeast, Victoria Cave near Settle, has produced remains of the former inhabitants of these now bare hillsides. Hippopotamus, lion, elephant and rhinoceros have all been found in the Lower Cave. Long extinct in Britain, these mammals were characteristic of the so-called 'hippopotamus fauna' which existed between Ice Ages when the climate was warmer than it is today.

The power of water erosion is visible throughout limestone areas, and perhaps one of the most spectacular results of it in England is the natural amphitheatre of Malham Cove, almost 100 metres (330 feet) high. This was carved out of the bedrock by a stream carrying water from Malham Tarn cascading over the wall made by the Craven Fault. The waterfall ceased when the stream found alternative underground routes, although it persisted intermittently during heavy floods. As recently as the early part of the

A fine example of the natural phenomenon of limestone pavement can be seen on Ingleborough's flanks.

last century the Tarn waters reached the lip of the Cove, but were dispersed in a huge spray before they reached the bottom.

Bare pavements – especially ones which are subjected to strong winds – are hardly conducive to a wide range of wildlife, but the plants and animals which do occur are well adapted to living in this inhospitable habitat. Plants which grow directly in contact with the pavement must be lime-loving or, at least, lime tolerant; there are places however where acid-loving plants grow on the limestone – on top of a peat layer. The lack of hedgerows and scrub greatly restricts the range of breeding birds, although wheatears use crevices in the man-made limestone walls, while meadow pipits, curlews, skylarks and lapwings nest in the grassy pastures.

Rabbits are not often to be seen, since they are most active at dusk and dawn, but their presence is confirmed by the droppings which they leave behind as they move from the surrounding pastures where they dig their burrows, on to the pavement areas to feed. There is also a much more intimate life among the grikes, including a curious little fungus which lives solely on rabbit droppings.

It is possible to walk over limestone pavement and not encounter any animals, yet a dewy morning may reveal spiders' webs stretched across the grikes, a wet day will bring out snails, while a warm day will lure out butterflies to feed on wild flowers. One glorious morning in early June I spotted a green-veined white flitting from one herb Robert flower to another, much more nimbly than I could attempt to reach it with a camera. I heard the distinctive 'drumming' call of a snipe, and out of the corner of my eye I saw a stoat streak across the top of the pavement and then vanish into a grike. Apart from rabbits and that single stoat I have never seen any other wild mammals while walking over limestone pavements, but the strange shapes of the rock and the plants hidden among them never fail to intrigue and delight me – whatever the weather.

SHIFTING SANDS

No part of Britain's coastline which is unprotected by man-made defences is a permanent feature. The coast is constantly changing as the sea erodes some parts of the shore and builds up others. Where the coast is rocky, this process is so slow that perceptible changes may take decades to occur, but where it is sandy, the time scale is much shorter. Spits, bars and dunes can sometimes be thrown up in just a few days, while winter gales can transform an idyllic holiday resort into a sandless bay overnight.

Old maps and historical records reveal a number of towns and even cities which have been engulfed by shifting sand or the encroaching sea. There are also many instances of coastal settlements becoming landlocked as new dunes distanced them from the shore. Harlech Castle, for example, was built in 1286 on top of cliffs above a harbour on the mid-Wales coast, but today, the castle lies nearly a kilometre (about half-a-mile) inland and is separated from the coastline by a sandy spit and dunes. Further south in Wales, the city of Kenfig was choked by sand at the end of the fifteenth century. All that remains today are outlines of a few walls just discernible beneath the sandy mantle. In Cornwall, shifting sands buried middens, a church, houses, and the tin-trading city of Langarrow, which stretched from Crantock to Perranporth in its heyday just after the end of the Bronze Age.

Sand, the agent of this change, consists of tiny rock fragments which have either been

Marram grass dominates the dunes at Ainsdale, binding together the wind-blown sand grains.

created by the erosion of coastal cliffs and stacks, or deposited by rivers carrying the particles in suspension from inland areas. Some of the sand may then be thrown up on shore, to be exposed at low tide. Once the sand dries out, it begins to move when subjected to winds of more than 16 km/h (10 mph). As soon as the wind drops, or an obstacle such as a piece of driftwood or strandline litter slows it down, the sand grains fall to the ground and build up to form a miniature dune on the seaward side of the obstacle.

Up and down the country, dunes are known by a variety of local names. They are *links* in Northumberland and Scotland, *meols* in Merseyside and Norfolk, *warrens* in Anglesey, *towans* in Cornwall and *burrows* in Devon, Somerset and South Wales. I always enjoy visiting dunes, because something new always turns up. It may be a plant not seen before or, more likely, the behaviour of an animal not previously observed. Dunes are built on such a scale that it is impossible to get to know every detailed part from a few casual visits. Also, the sameness of the young dunes makes it difficult to remember which bits have already been explored.

The extensive north Merseyside dunes – the fourth largest area in Britain – have developed from sand eroded from the Pennine Hills and carried by the River Mersey into Liverpool Bay, to be mixed up with sea shell fragments and later dumped by the incoming tide on the shore. During the summer, the sand dries out at the top of the beach and when the prevailing westerly winds blow, it gets carried some distance inland, depending on the force of the

The sea bindweed's spreading shape and small fleshy leaves suit it well to the dry life among the marram grass and on the open sand.

wind. Remains of sea shells make these dunes lime-rich, which encourages the growth of lime-loving plants such as blue fleabane, ploughman's spikenard, carline thistle and felwort or autumn gentian, which are just as at home here as on chalk grassland.

However, before these plants can grow the sand must be stabilised by 'pioneer' plants with deeply penetrating roots which anchor them in the shifting sand. Walking inland from the sea along the Nature Trail across the Ainsdale Dunes you can see this process unfolding. A clear succession of dune ridges runs parallel to the shore line, beginning nearest the sea with

the young embryo dunes with only a few hardy pioneer plants. Behind them are the older fixed dunes with a much greater range of flowers and shrubs, and finally, furthest from the sea are the pine woods planted from 1914 onwards.

The first step in binding together the sand of an embryo dune is taken when two grasses – sand couch and lime grass – which both tolerate a sea water wetting, take root on the dune's seaward side.

Today, as fast as new dunes are built up at Ainsdale they are being destroyed by the equipment used to remove the abundant rubbish discarded by thousands of holidaymakers. More recently, a change of tactics has been adopted, and instead of removing the debris (and much sand as well), it is pushed up in front of the embryo dunes in the hope that it will get submerged by wind-blown sand in the summer.

Marram grass, a later arrival which cannot survive dousing with sea water, is the champion dune builder. Even when completely buried by fresh sand it sends up new shoots and leaves, helping to trap still more sand. Underground creeping stems as well as deep roots help both to anchor the plants and to hold the dune's shape. Marram grass has been protected since the sixteenth century, when it was made a criminal offence to uproot it. A few miles south of Ainsdale, at Formby, the dunes have eroded inland, no doubt helped by locals unwittingly cutting marram grass during the winter months for making into mats, brushes and brooms.

Although embryo dunes are literally a stone's-throw from the sea, they can be very dry, and the plants that grow on them have to survive with very little water, often in quite salty conditions. Many do this by having leaves that lose only small amounts of water through evaporation. All over the surface of their leaves most plants have microscopic pores or stomata, through which water is lost by evaporation, but marram grass has stomata confined to ridges inside the curving leaf. In dry weather the leaves roll up into tight tubes, reducing the water loss to the minimum. There are other ways in which sand dune plants conserve water: the sea sandwort stores water in fleshy succulent leaves; the sea storksbill has a dense mat of fine hair covering the leaves; the sea holly has spiny leaves with a thick waxy coating and tap roots up to 2 metres (6 feet) long.

These water-saving devices often have quite an effect on the appearance of the plants. It seems hard to believe that the savage-looking sea holly is related to parsley. In Elizabethan times, the roots of sea holly were candied with sugar and orange flower water and sold as eringoes (from the Latin name *Eryngium*). The eringoe trade was centred on Colchester in Essex where they were sold for more than two

centuries as a remedy for nervous disorders. In the West Country, the young shoots of sea holly were once eaten like asparagus.

As the embryo dune develops some of the original plants begin to die, and the resulting layer of humus makes the sand more fertile. Conditions are now suitable for a much wider range of plants including mosses, which help to bind the surface sand, and also shrubs like the sea buckthorn. This was originally planted to help stabilise Ainsdale dunes around the turn of the century. It has now spread extensively – both by suckers and by seed – often forming dense thickets. Although it prevents other plants from growing beneath it, it does provide shelter and nesting sites for birds such as blackbirds and whitethroats, as well as dens for foxes. In winter, flocks of redwings and fieldfares feast on the sea buckthorn's ripe orange berries. Like most dune plants, it is very tenacious. Rabbits used to keep it in check, but after the outbreak of myxomatosis and also following the drought in the middle of the 1970s, sea buckthorn spread rapidly. It cannot be controlled by

The sharp prickly leaves of the sea holly serve both to conserve water and to deter browsing animals.

cutting, because the cut stems simply resprout from their base.

Those younger dunes which are well out of the reach of the sea support two conspicuous yellow-flowered plants. Evening primrose sports large showy flowers which open within a few minutes as the temperature falls at dusk and quickly fade in the heat of the following day. Although in normal light the flowers are a uniform yellow, when they are photographed in ultra-violet light, they show a spectacular pattern similar to the visible colourful streaks on pansy flowers. This ultra-violet light pattern, normally invisible to our eyes, acts together with a nectar secretion, to attract night-flying moths to visit the flowers and, hopefully, to cross-pollinate them.

Ragwort, which has smaller, less conspicuous yellow flowers, soon spreads on to dunes by way of its wind-borne seed parachutes. Its flowers are visited by day-flying moths such as the 6-spot burnet moth and by butterflies. Any part of ragwort – the flowers, leaves and even the stems – are fodder for cinnabar moth caterpillars, whose black and gold striped colouration should surely make them the mascot of Wolverhampton Wanderers! Although the distinctive warning colouration makes the caterpillars very conspicuous, they survive attack from predatory birds by having an unpleasant taste. When a young bird attacks a caterpillar it learns to associate the bold colours with the noxious taste and thereafter to leave it well alone, as it does with the black and red adult moth. This same method of survival can also be seen in the stinging wasps, and even in the harmless yellow and black wasp beetle which protects itself by mimicking their distinctive coloration.

The older, fixed dunes furthest from the sea can be distinguished from young mobile dunes not only by their larger number of plant species but also by the grey colour of their sand. But even these dunes are susceptible to erosion, especially if the plants are damaged by repeated trampling, or worse still, by beach-buggies. If dry dunes catch fire, the plants will be destroyed, and once the surface cover is broken, wind starts to eat away at the bare sand, and ultimately a huge hollow – known as a blow-out – can develop. If no further trampling takes place marram grass may gradually invade and help to rebuild the dune, but often man has to lend a helping hand either by planting marram grass seedlings, or by erecting brushwood fences – sea buckthorn is used at Ainsdale – to help trap moving sand.

One of the best ways of finding out what kinds of animals live on dunes is to get up early in the morning and look at their tracks in the bare sand, before they have been obliterated by wind or by human footprints. Large tracks, made by birds such as gulls or terns stand out most easily, but if you are a keen observer, you will gradually be able to build up a detailed picture of animal activity betweeen dusk and dawn. Clusters of four rounded tracks are the mark of a hopping rabbit; parallel lines are made by a crawling cinnabar caterpillar; while a line running through the middle of small tracks is made by a lizard dragging its tail. The abrupt ending of a rabbit's track where it intersects another, coupled with scuffling, may mark the site of a fox's kill; whereas an impression of outstretched wingtips will indicate an aerial predator, such as an owl, has swooped down to make its attack.

At sunrise, when there is dew on the ground, or during a rain shower, snails will be much in evidence crawling over plants with their outstretched tentacles. On a wet day in late June, I saw the flowering spikes of marram grass bent right over from the weight of several banded snails crawling over them.

An interesting part of a dune system probably least visited by humans is where small damp hollows and valleys known as slacks have developed. Here, an accumulation of humus and an impervious subsoil both help to retain water, encouraging the growth of plants unable to survive on the dry dune tops. In many slacks the ground remains damp in summer and the hollows are water-filled in winter. In spring and early summer, marsh plants are in flower in the slacks including wild orchids, brookweed, grass of Parnassus, marsh cinquefoil and creeping willow with its tiny yellow catkins. Although only reaching a height of 1 metre (3 feet) or less, creeping willow can form quite dense growths as a direct result of the reduced number of rabbits feeding on it in recent years.

An arctic tern examines its nesting site after a marathon migration from the seas off southern Africa.

Some slacks contain quite large pools where aquatic plants flourish, notably the long spikes of bulrush, bogbean, yellow flag, water plantain and water mint. Water beetles, water boatmen, and the nymphs of damselflies, mayflies and caddisflies live in the water itself. The shallow pools are prime breeding sites for amphibians. As well as common frogs and toads, the much rarer natterjack toad breeds in the Lancashire dune slacks. This toad, which has a distinctive yellow stripe down its back, lives only in sandy coastal sites where there are shallow pools suitable for breeding. Afforestation and urban development have resulted in the loss of over 80 per cent of these breeding sites in Britain during this century, major factors which have contributed to the natterjack now being specially protected by law. In recent years, new

scrapes have been dug in the Merseyside dunes to provide more breeding sites for these rare toads, and wet slacks which have been filled with sand have been re-excavated. The natterjack has short hind limbs which it uses to run rather than hop, which has earned it the alternative name of running toad. It breeds in late spring, and the loud croaking call of the males can be heard at dusk. Once the spawn ropes are laid, the eggs develop quickly, and the small toads appear in only 4–8 weeks. During winter, the toads hibernate in the sand.

Man has caused some dramatic and far-reaching changes – some now irreversible – to dune systems. The planting of extensive stands of pine trees which have a high water demand, lowers the water table. Heavy shade cast on the ground creates a sombre setting where only a few wild flowers are able to grow. Even under natural conditions, duneland plants and animals live with the threat of sudden, and possibly devastating, changes as storms shift the loose sand. Now roads have brought dunes within easy reach of anyone who has a car, and the combined disturbance of thousands of pairs of feet trampling over a confined area may have disastrous consequences. The thin layer of vegetation over the older dunes is all that keeps them stable, and if this is damaged the sand is easily moved elsewhere, disrupting the dune life which will take years to recover.

This photograph, taken by flash, captures a nocturnal natterjack toad swimming among marsh pennywort in its dune slack breeding pool.

A RIBBON OF LIFE

The Derwent, which drains the North Yorkshire Moors and the Vales of Pickering and York, is one of the cleanest rivers in Britain. Although it is tapped to provide drinking water for over a million people, it is also a haven for wildlife. The reason for the Derwent's lush banks is that the river's waters are both clear and rich in calcium – ideal conditions for plants. Many of these plants are characteristic of southern chalk rivers like the Test and Itchen, and in the Derwent they are at the northernmost limit of their distribution.

In the river itself, there are plants such as the starwort, which grows underwater in elongated clumps sending neat rosettes of bright green leaves to the surface, and the attractive water crowfoot, which has darker green, finely-branched underwater stems and leaves which snake gently in the current. Early in summer the crowfoot ribbons are dotted with white flowers which open as soon as the buds break the surface. When the river is not in spate, the clear water allows plenty of light to reach the submerged plants which grow vigorously to provide both food and shelter for a myriad of aquatic life, from nymphs of damselflies, stoneflies and mayflies to caddis larvae, water shrimps and water lice.

One of my favourite stretches of the Derwent is the part which flows through Forge Valley (see A woodland wakes p.7). It is here that the river has carved out a spectacular gorge, now clothed in woodland, forming a striking contrast with

As it passes through Forge Valley, the River Derwent flows past verdant banks fringed with ferns.

the flat rolling agricultural land through which the Derwent flows further south. From March through to August, the banks of the Derwent in Forge Valley sport an array of wild flowers which flourish in wet ground. Late in March, pinkish flowering spikes of butterbur thrust up through the ground before the leaves appear. The powerfully scented flowers, with their copious nectar supplies, attract both bees and butterflies at a time when the choice of flowers is limited. Long after the flowers have withered, the leaves continue growing until they reach the size of a small umbrella or sunshade – indeed, chickens will seek their shade on hot, sunny days. Before the days of refrigerators, butterbur leaves were wrapped around butter to keep it cool. Shortly after the butterbur flowers appear, and persisting well into June, there is one of the finest displays of marsh marigolds, or kingcups, I have ever seen. A plant of wet and waterlogged places, marsh marigold has suffered greatly in recent years as a result of extensive land drainage all over Britain.

No other plant quite matches up to the spectacular display of the marsh marigolds, although clumps of pink cuckoo flowers (which open around the time that the cuckoo returns to Britain from its over-wintering grounds in Africa), cream lady's mantle, blue water forget-me-not and mauve water mint all help to complement the lush green ferns, sedges and grasses which thrive beside the Derwent.

During the summer, several families of mallard can be seen swimming amongst crowfoot, the fluffy balls of up-ended ducklings drifting along the current as they feed. Where the river

The large pink spikes of butterbur flowers are a valuable source of nectar for insects in early spring.

flows out of the North Yorkshire Moors National Park, near the end of Forge Valley, its banks are not nearly so lush since they are trampled much more and it is here that mallards often lie out on the bank resting.

Kingfishers breed along some stretches of the Derwent, including Forge Valley, but a flash of steel blue may be all you will glimpse of this shy bird. Most people when they first see a kingfisher are disappointed with its small size, but what it lacks in size it more than makes up with its colourful plumage. The underside is chestnut, the throat and neck are white, while the head, back and wings are a blue-green colour which varies depending on the angle of the light. Such brilliant colours are more typical of tropical birds, and the family to which the kingfisher belongs is indeed predominantly a tropical one. An adult kingfisher can be sexed by the colour of the bill; in a male it is all black, whereas the female has a dark orange patch below. Both birds use their tough bills to dig out the nest tunnel in the riverside bank. When the tunnel is 1 metre (3 feet) long, the round white eggs are laid at the end. Once the young kingfishers hatch, their parents are kept busy diving for fish – usually bullheads or sticklebacks – which are stunned by repeatedly beating them against a perch. Kingfishers, which are badly hit by severe winters and by river pollution, now have special protection in Britain. Anyone wishing to photograph these birds at, or near, their nests must first gain approval from the Nature Conservancy Council.

Otters, water voles and water shrews share the banks of the Derwent with the kingfisher. All these mammals are rather secretive, especially the otter which is usually nocturnal except in remote undisturbed areas such as Shetland and the west coast of Scotland, where it has become totally marine. Otters are now very rare in most of their original inland sites. Loss of habitat, disturbance and pollution have probably all contributed to the decline of this carnivore which feeds mainly on fish – including eels, trout and salmon – as well as on crayfish. But,

Sitting on a favourite vantage point, a kingfisher waits for passing fish which it catches by plunging into the water and seizing it in its bill.

after a snowfall, it is still well worth looking out for otter tracks and slides – one of the best ways of detecting their presence.

Unlike the otter, the water vole is active both day and night and can be seen swimming short distances or sitting on its haunches browsing on succulent stems close by its bankside burrow. Also known as the water rat, it feeds on

Each April, the bare banks of the River Dove in Farndale are transformed when the wild daffodils flower.

freshwater snails and mussels as well. The water shrew has a characteristic long nose with highly sensitive hairs, but it can be distinguished from other shrews by the black upper coat and the white belly. Like all shrews, it must feed frequently throughout each day just to stay alive. Aquatic larvae, snails and worms are killed by its venomous saliva.

Freshwater snails and crayfish both flourish in the waters of the Derwent because calcium is essential for the maintenance of their hard

shells. Crayfish, which look like miniature lobsters, move by walking leisurely over the river bed but they can suddenly escape backwards by rapidly flicking the tail beneath the body. They use their powerful pair of pincers to grasp food and to crack open snail shells.

The Derwent collects several tributaries on its way southwards. One is the River Dove which flows through the picturesque 'daffodil dale' of Farndale. Here, tens of thousands of people converge for a few short weeks each spring to feast their eyes on the yellow ribbons of wild daffodils running along the banks for mile upon mile. No written account can quite prepare you for the sheer excitement of seeing so many nodding blooms. They were threatened by a scheme to build a reservoir but fortunately they are now completely protected within a local nature reserve. The daffodils are speedily dispersed to new downstream sites when the river undercuts its banks, unearthing bulbs, and later dumping its load among protruding alder roots.

Downstream, the Derwent is often tranquil and overgrown, but it begins life as a tiny acidic peaty stream swiftly tumbling down the hillsides. Before the last Ice Age it flowed eastwards out to the sea in Scalby Bay north of Scarborough, but as the ice sheets built up, the Derwent's outlet was cut off by a huge ice wall. Even then, after the ice began to melt in the summer months, the route remained blocked by the wall of glacial rubbish left behind as boulder clay cliffs. The Derwent's impounded waters formed Troutsdale Lake, a large glacial lake similar to the ones which can still be seen in Iceland today. When water from the south of Troutsdale Lake overflowed it gouged out a channel along a natural fault between limestone and sandstone outcrops. This new route for the Derwent turned it through 90 degrees, and, by diverting it inland when it was only 6 kilometres (3·5 miles) from the sea, greatly added to its length. The force of the waters cut

In late evening, this banded agrion, a type of damselfly, has ceased flying up and down the riverbank and taken refuge in the safety of the waterside reeds.

into the land creating the gorge now known as Forge Valley. Further south, Kirkham Abbey Gorge is another overflow channel cut by the waters of the glacial Lake Pickering as the Derwent forged its way relentlessly southwards, ultimately meandering across the Vale of York until it met the Ouse for the final part of its roundabout journey to the sea.

More recently, man has manipulated the Derwent waters, notably by making the Sea Cut high upriver at Hackness, and by constructing a barrage and lock to keep out sea water downstream near the confluence with the Ouse. The

A party of mallards feeds among the watercress that spreads out from the Derwent's banks in early summer.

Sea Cut was dug entirely by hand during the first decade of the last century as an overflow channel to carry the flood water generated by heavy storms, or after a sudden thaw of snowclad moors, out to the sea at Scalby Ness. The Cut, which follows the old route of the Derwent, falls 44 metres in 8 kilometres (145 feet in 5 miles) over a series of eight weirs and emerges through cliffs of boulder clay – a legacy of the ice sheets. Before the Cut was dug, the Derwent was unable to contain the flood waters

which often overflowed the banks carrying away livestock and flooding riverside farms. In any river the rate of flow will vary greatly throughout the year, but it is particularly dramatic in the River Derwent.

Visitors will most often see the river in a restful mood gently moving the waterweeds to and fro, but this peaceful scene becomes dramatically transformed when the river is in spate. Then, raging silt-laden brown flood waters tear at banks flattening marginal plants and ripping branches off submerged plants. Yet life in the river is remarkably resilient and is, indeed, better adapted to survive natural disasters than man-made pollutants, so it soon recovers and the peaceful scene returns once more, with remnants of debris caught on branches of overhanging alders clearly marking the highest flood level. Downstream, in the low-lying Vale of York, the land used to be perpetually waterlogged until embankments were built and drainage ditches dug so as to prevent summer flooding of agricultural lands, but the lower Derwent has traditionally flooded meadowland between Wheldrake and Bubwith in winter. Known as Ings, these flooded water-meadows attract so many wildfowl (notably Bewick's swans, wigeon, teal, pochard and mallard) in the winter, that they are regarded as a wetland site of international importance and the area is now one of the Yorkshire Naturalists' Trust reserves. During drier spells, the grassy Ings, enriched by the silt carried down during the winter floods are grazed by cattle, and in summer they are cut for hay.

Over the centuries, parts of the river have been straightened to aid navigation. The lower stretches of the Derwent were navigable as long ago as the Middle Ages, but a series of locks and weirs had to be built for boats to reach as far as Malton. The recently-built tidal barrage now prevents salt water from the Ouse entering the Derwent, providing an even greater volume of fresh water for domestic and industrial use and ensuring the diversity of river life is maintained, since only a very limited number of species will tolerate living in even slightly saline water.

What does the future hold for this beautiful river? Recent changes to the water system include an increase in pleasure boat traffic (and the appearance of some illegal mooring sites), and the tidal barrage has caused spring flooding of riverside meadows. Conservationists, naturalists, farmers and anglers are all very concerned about future changes to the Derwent which could so easily threaten the natural pattern of life within its varied habitats.

Up and down the country, man has left his mark on rivers; by straightening banks he destroys nesting sites and cover for many birds, by building weirs and dams he blocks the natural migrations of fish, by tapping rivers for irrigating his crops he may lower the water level, while pollution of the water may result in large scale fish mortalities. Hopefully, the future of the Derwent will be safeguarded through hindsight of the problems that have beset many other British rivers.

A SEABIRD SANCTUARY

Jutting out into the North Sea between Filey and Bridlington Bays on the Yorkshire coast, the huge chalk promontory of Flamborough Head has claimed the lives of many seafarers who misjudged the position of their ships. For centuries attempts have been made to alert shipping to this rocky promontory, initially by means of a flaming beacon (which may have inspired the name of the headland) and later by a lighthouse.

Today in autumn and early spring when sea mists frequently envelope Flamborough, all natural sounds become obliterated by the double blast of the foghorn every 90 seconds. In the days before the foghorn was installed, exploding rockets were let off at five-minute intervals, soaring high above the cliffs. But ten centuries ago when the Vikings invaded Flamborough, they would have encountered a headland enlivened only by the sounds of the crashing sea, the cries of the seabirds, and maybe the high-pitched squeaks of a dolphin following their long-boats inshore.

The imposing chalk cliffs are full of surprises. Although a walk along the cliff-top path illustrates well the destructive powers of the sea, the cliffs, gullies, caves, stacks and arches carved by this natural sculptor are perhaps best seen from a boat or a small plane. Only then can you appreciate the majestic panorama of the 76-metre (250-foot) high cliffs plunging into the sea and begin to sense how they inspired many legends about smuggling, with the numerous

At Flamborough Head, rain, frost and waves have carved dramatic arches and caves from the soft chalk of the cliffs.

caves providing safe hideaways from the arm of the law.

Caves begin life as cracks or weak points at the bottom of cliffs, which are enlarged by waves dashing against them. As the sea undercuts the cliffs, falls of chalky rubble crash on to the beach. Flamborough's chalk cliffs are also attacked by acid rain water. The sea quickly takes advantage of caverns and crevasses created in this way, enlarging them still further into sizeable caves. If the sea carves out a cave on both sides of a headland, so that the two meet, an overhead arch is formed as can be seen at North Sea Landing and Kindle Scar in Yorkshire, or at Durdle Door in Dorset. These dramatic features are, alas, not permanent ones, for an archway slowly erodes away until it eventually breaks right through leaving a vertical rocky column, or stack, cut off from the mainland. The Needles, a particularly famous line of chalk stacks which run out to sea from the west coast of the Isle of Wight, are the remnants of a ridge which connected the Isle of Wight with the Dorset mainland until some 8,000 years ago.

Offshore stacks are always popular sites for breeding seabirds, because they are usually inaccessible to man. In summer, the distinctive piercing cries of gulls and kittiwakes can be heard from their nest sites on stacks and cliffs around Flamborough. Distinguished as the only gull with black legs, the kittiwake is also the only one which can nest on narrow ledges of precipitous cliffs. As it utters its 'kittee-waak' call, it reveals a brilliant red gape inside its yellow bill.

A 6·5-kilometre (4-mile) walk northwards along the coastal footpath crosses Danes' Dyke, a huge natural ravine and man-made rampart built in prehistoric times, and leads to Bempton Cliffs, an RSPB reserve established to protect a variety of nesting seabirds including puffins, razorbills and fulmars (known as 'mallies' by the local fishermen) as well as Britain's sole mainland colony of gannets. A closer look at the ledges shows that each kind of bird has a distinct preference for its nest site. The dainty kittiwakes cement their cup-shaped nests created from a mixture of bird droppings, mud

A pair of kittiwakes reacts to danger by displaying their strikingly coloured throats.

and green seaweeds, on short, narrow ledges, while the more cumbersome gannets select the wider ledges. Guillemots make no nest at all, laying their pear-shaped eggs on bare rocky ledges, while puffins nest in the deeper crevices.

To experience for the first time the sight and sound of seabirds expertly wheeling and gliding past their breeding cliff face is almost unreal. The individual sounds mix harmoniously together into a complete orchestra, and like most visitors to bird cliffs I find it is easy to forget all sense of time and simply stand and marvel at the spectacle.

But it has not always been like this at Bempton. Imagine, if you can, the sound of gunfire echoing off the cliffs as men shot at the seabirds both from the cliff tops and from boats at sea. Kittiwakes suffered most in the past because their feathers were prized to create fashionable hats. Seeing the 30,000 pairs nesting at Bempton today under complete protection, it is hard to believe that in the last century they were reduced to such low numbers, that it proved no longer worthwhile exploiting them. Nationwide census counts made in 1959 and 1969, show that the British kittiwake population increased by almost 50 per cent over this ten-year period. Kittiwakes now nest all round Britain wherever there are precipitous cliff sites. They even use windowsills of coastal warehouses in Northumberland and County Durham which, like the natural cliffs, have vertical walls with narrow ledges; further south, they have commandeered the Pier Pavilion at Lowestoft in Suffolk as a nest site.

As well as shooting the birds at Bempton, for over 250 years men descended on ropes from the top of the 120-metre (400-foot) high cliffs to collect an annual harvest of as many as 130,000

It will take five years for this fledgling gannet (right) to develop fully the dramatic white, yellow and black plumage of adulthood.

seabird eggs – mostly those of guillemots. This practice was known locally as 'climming'. Each team worked their own piece of cliff face during the period from mid-May to the end of June. Two or three men used a pulley or winch to lower down the climmer who wore a tin hat for protection from falling rocks as he collected the eggs in a canvas bag. Climming was finally prohibited by the passing of the 1954 Protection of Birds Act.

As the tide ebbs away below the cliffs, rocky platforms – remnants of past cliffs – can be seen extending down the shore. I can never resist the chance of following a receding tide down the beach to explore some of the life which occurs between the tides. This boundary between land and sea is a zone of continual change, for here gulls may walk in search of a stranded starfish only hours after fish swam up rocky gulleys. The relentless rhythm of the tides is linked with the relative positions of the earth, the moon and the sun. When there is a new or a full moon, the sun and moon lie roughly in line with each other, exerting an increased gravitational force, causing the high-ranging 'spring tides' to occur once a fortnight throughout the year. Alternating with the spring tides are the small-ranging 'neap' tides which do not reach so high up or recede so low down the shore.

Forays on to the shore are much more exciting during the spring tides, for then a greater part of the lower shore is exposed for exploration. Barnacles, limpets, winkles and seaweeds, all permanent inhabitants of the intertidal zone, have to tolerate a relentless tidal rhythm, alternately exposing them to air or submerging them beneath the sea. In winter, they are bathed in seawater temperatures only a few degrees above freezing, while on a hot summer's day, the surface temperature of rocks can exceed 40°C (104°F).

Barnacles permanently anchor themselves to rocks to withstand buffeting by the sea. When exposed to air they keep themselves moist by closing up their outer shells, but once submerged the shells open and they start feeding on microscopic planktonic organisms which they filter from the sea water. At first glance barnacles look very similar to small limpets, but in fact they are related to crabs and lobsters. A barnacle starts life as a free-swimming larva. After months of drifting in the sea as part of the plankton it drops down from the surface waters, settles and cements itself to a rock face, and is there for life. Like earthworms, barnacles are hermaphrodite animals – each individual functioning as both male and female, but they none the less need to mate with another individual to ensure each other's eggs are fertilized. It is therefore essential for a barnacle to make sure it settles adjacent to a prospective mate – otherwise it will inevitably lead a completely monastic life. Existing barnacles secrete a chemical substance which the larva detects and homes in on.

A limpet is well adapted to withstand attacking waves; its conical shell offers little resistance to the sea, while its large muscular foot can clamp so tightly to the rock it can be impossible to dislodge. Just before a limpet is uncovered by the ebbing tide, it stops crawling around, pulling its shell tightly on to the rock so that the soft body is kept moist. When submerged though, a limpet will crawl around on its muscular foot using a toothed sandpaper-like 'tongue' to rasp small seaweeds or microscopic algae growing as a film on the rock surface. In whatever direction a limpet moves on these feeding forays, it is able to home in again on its own little' patch of rock where its shell makes a perfect fit. You may wonder how a limpet finds its way home. Before the tide turns, it backtracks along its feeding trail sensing a chemical left behind. It may sometimes take a short cut home, possibly by recognising the surface features of the rock immediately around its home territory. On beaches such as the chalky rock platform at Flamborough, where the rock is relatively soft, the limpet grinds a distinct 'scar' in the rock as it repeatedly rotates its shell to get a good fit. When a limpet dies, it drops off the rock revealing its scar as a miniature crater which provides a sheltered home for a host of small snails, as well as young limpets.

Flamborough women used to collect limpets or 'flithers' as bait for their fishermen to use. The women would go to any lengths to get their bait: being lowered down the cliffs by rope or shuffling down an icy slope in winter on their bottoms. When we venture on to the shore

In a rock pool shared by a shore crab and a limpet, a circular scar marks an old limpet home.

today, we dress for the occasion, but Flamborough fisherwomen had to hitch up their long skirts to keep them dry. For hundreds of years, fishermen operating between the Tweed and the Humber rivers went to sea in brightly-coloured open boats known as 'cobles'. Before the First World War, some seventy cobles operated from Flamborough alone, to catch cod, skate, ling, haddock, catfish or halibut on lines in winter, crabs in pots at Easter-time and herring in late summer. The catch was loaded into baskets strapped astride donkeys which carried their heavy loads up the steep path from the beach to the village.

A walk down on to any rocky shore at low tide will reveal that no single animal or seaweed lives over the entire shore; instead each kind is restricted to a distinct level or zone. Only a few

Buoyed up by coastal updraughts, gannets glide majestically past their breeding cliffs.

organisms, including tiny winkles, are able to survive the conditions right at the top shore where they are exposed to the air for many hours each day. Lower down the shore, however, the number of species increases, for here the shore is bathed by the sea for a much longer period each day. Exposed rocky shores which are constantly buffeted by waves are not nearly such rich hunting grounds as sheltered ones. Even along the same stretch of coastline, no two shores have identical angles of slope, and sizes or shapes of crevices and rock pools. The variation in 'micro' habitats influences where different animals choose to live. Uneven weathering of Flamborough's chalk cliffs provides numerous hideaways for winkles, while elongated crevices in the rocky platform on the beach retain sea water after the tide has ebbed down the shore.

Reflections of sky and clouds on the water surface of these miniature natural aquaria make it difficult to see clearly the different kinds of pool life, unless you wear Polaroid sunglasses. All anglers know the value of these glasses for revealing the whereabouts of lurking fish; I often use a polarizing filter over my camera lens to get clearer pictures of life beneath the surface.

Soft-bodied sea anemones, prawns and fish may be seen, all of which can continue feeding until the incoming tide floods the shore again. Yet living in a pool – especially one high up on the shore – can be fraught with hazards. On a hot summer's day the shallow water can gradually warm up to be suddenly flushed out by the cool incoming tide, which must be akin to plunging in a cold bath after taking a hot shower.

Even if the incoming tide drives you up off the beach in summer you can always walk along the cliff-top path searching for coastal flowers.

The white chalk cliffs at Flamborough are capped with a layer of soft boulder clay which was carried down by Ice Age glaciers, and is now covered with turf so that it appears like a white cake topped with green icing. Amongst the turf, colourful flowers stand out like jewels. Even when a landslip erodes away part of a cliff, thrift or sea pink hangs on by the tip of its long tap root, while the narrow leaves and their tufted arrangement both help to reduce loss of water caused by drying winds. Although we always associate the pink bobbles of thrift with the smell of the sea, this robust plant can withstand the freezing summit of Ben Nevis every bit as well as the rigours of a salt water shower. While a dousing of sea water would kill most garden plants, cliff flowers are well adapted to the changeable coastal weather. The contrasts are great; a sunny day with a clear blue sky can suddenly be transformed into one with leaden skies and gale-force winds which deter even the gulls from taking to the air. In January 1953 when 100-knot winds raged, they whipped the salt spray 60 metres (200 feet) above the sea. Yet shore and cliff life is remarkably resilient to climatic extremes.

From the cliff-top paths, binoculars are useful for searching out plants growing on lower inaccessible ledges as well as for spotting birds at sea. Seabirds pass by the Flamborough coast at almost any time of year. After the spring invasion of breeding seabirds, sandwich terns, Arctic skuas and small flocks of waders pass by, while autumn is the season for shearwaters. If you are prepared to spend time scanning the sea surface, there is always the chance of spotting a diver, a great skua or a sooty shearwater. The cliffs themselves are spectacular at any time of year; their colours change from dawn to dusk and whenever a cloud shields the sun, making a constantly varying pattern of light and shade through which the birds glide and turn.

TIME AND TIDE IN AN ESTUARY

Apparently bleak and inhospitable, estuaries can none the less be evocative and haunting places. Huge expanses of mud flats, exposed twice daily by the ebbing tide, resound with the calls of nimble-footed waders. For humans, however, walking is quite hazardous since the fine mud, with a consistency of ever-deepening custard, threatens to retain a boot at each step.

Life in estuaries has to withstand not only turbid silty waters brought down by rivers and variable tidal levels, but also changes in currents and salinity. It is therefore not surprising that the number of different kinds of animals which live permanently in estuaries is quite limited. But the mud banks and tidal marshes are so highly productive that their animals and plants generate energy, in the form of living matter, up to seven times greater than the same area of a field of wheat. Vast numbers of microscopic bacteria grow by extracting nitrogen from the atmosphere, providing food in turn for dense concentrations of marine invertebrates – worms, crustaceans and molluscs all occur in the mud. Up to 100,000 ragworms have been found in one square metre (11 square feet). It is small wonder therefore that many of our estuaries are vitally important overwintering places for waders which congregate in huge flocks to feed at this time of year.

During summer many of the birds have left, and it is the flowers that are now at their best. Most grow in the saltmarsh which develops in the upper parts of sheltered tidal reaches of an estuary. Here, plants have to tolerate being wetted, or even submerged, by salty water, and many of them bloom late in summer when there are no high-ranging spring tides which would swamp their flowers and prevent pollination taking place.

Saltmarshes occur all round Britain, with some of the finest stretches being on the north Norfolk coast around Blakeney. Quite by chance, I wandered onto the saltmarsh bordering the Lune estuary on the Lancashire coast, when I walked down off the disused railway line which runs across it. This area is typical of many such marshes and has a variety of plants as well as its quota of creeks and salt pans.

On the landward edge of a saltmarsh where the plants completely carpet the mud, walking is quite safe. But, snaking their way through the stable ground are the treacherous mud-lined channels which drain away brackish water after high tides. The fast rate of flow prevents flowering plants from establishing themselves on the mud which is soft and very deep. From the air, saltmarsh creeks form an intricate pattern, rather like veins, as they weave their way out into the main channels. At ground level, they can often be detected from a distance by the grey-green bands of sea purslane which prefers growing on the slightly raised ground bordering the creeks. As the tide ebbs, exposing the muddy channels, birds move in to feed. In the summer, I have seen black-headed gulls,

The sun beams down onto the sea behind a flock of knots overwintering in an estuary.

mallard, shelduck and flocks of young starlings feeding in the Lune estuary channels.

The plants which grow on the flat ground between the creeks may vary from one locality to another, but they most often include thrift or sea pink, sea lavender, sea aster, cord grass and glasswort – the last two tending to dominate the younger parts of the saltmarsh where bare mud is still much in evidence. Here, as on sand dunes, a succession of plants, beginning with the quickly-spreading pioneers, colonises the mud flats, helping to trap more silt as they take root and become established.

Glasswort, also known as marsh samphire, is a plant which grows from seed every year and

Despite their small size, the massed flowers of the sea lavender make a sheet of colour in a saltmarsh.

At Sunderland Point on the Lune estuary, cord grass is the first plant to spread over the soft mud.

has segmented succulent stems and tiny flowers. From the time of the sixteenth century, glasswort plants were dried and burnt to obtain the sodium ash needed for glass-making. Young glasswort plants used to be eaten raw in salads, while older plants were cooked. Even today, glasswort can be bought alongside other vegetables on some East Anglian market stalls, although it is no longer used in the manufacture of glass.

The prime pioneer mud-binders, however, are the cord grasses which, being perennial plants, do not die at the end of each autumn and so can continue sprouting anew from their underground stems. The most vigorous cord grass

originated in Southampton Water as a hybrid, or cross, between a British species and an American one. No other plant in Britain builds up mud flats and reclaims land from the sea so efficiently as this hybrid cord grass. It has spread very rapidly around our coasts, accelerated by man's own deliberate introductions to many areas, including Hightown and Southport on the Lancashire coast.

In spring, pink bobbles of thrift colour the marsh. Also at this time, scurvy grass produces its white flowers. Before citrus fruits were imported to our country, scurvy grass was used as an invaluable source of Vitamin C for sailors on long sea voyages, to prevent the disease from which the plant takes its name.

Late in summer, when sheets of sea lavender flower, the marsh is a purple haze of colour. The flattened heads of tiny flowers are unusual in that the brightly-coloured scales which surround each one continue to attract insects such as bees and butterflies even after the tiny petals have withered. The daisy-like flowers of sea aster, with their purple petals surrounding a yellow centre, may seem like a less spectacular version of the cultivated Michaelmas daisies, but they still make a showy display among the predominantly green growth on the marsh. They were particularly popular with the Elizabethans who even went to the trouble of adding crushed rocksalt to their gardens so sea asters would grow there. The caterpillars of the star-wort moth often can be found feeding on sea aster, and they will also feed on cultivated asters and Michaelmas daisies.

Distinctive features of the middle part of the salt marsh are the circular-shaped salt pans, which are formed when small drainage channels become blocked at either end. When sea water floods over the marsh it fills the pans, gradually

This shore crab is one of the few kinds of crab able to survive in brackish estuarine waters.

evaporating to produce highly salty water in which few, if any, plants can grow. During hot spells, the bare mud cracks to form stress patterns as it dries out.

The upper limit of each tide is clearly marked by a line of debris, but nowadays discarded plastic objects and pieces of polystyrene feature all too often among the natural clumps of seaweed and wood. Shells of the shore crab also abound among saltmarsh strandlines, for this crab will tolerate living in salinities as low as 6 parts per thousand, about one-sixth of that of sea water. The crab's hard outer skeleton prevents it from growing slowly and continuously; instead it grows in fits and starts by shedding (moulting) its hard shell, which may be carried away by the currents. The new shell is at first soft, so the body can grow to fill it, but once the shell has hardened, the crab remains this size until the next moult. At the landward edge of the marsh, once the salinity drops below 5 parts per thousand, the salt marsh plants are replaced by reeds and rushes, and the estuary's coastal character fades away.

On the northern bank of the Lune Estuary is Sunderland Point, once the old sea port for Lancaster. Now it is a lonely headland, the port having shrunk after losing its trade to the dock on the southern bank. Sunderland Point is a fascinating place, not least because its causeway is flooded during high spring tides when the community is completely cut off by road. In the early part of the eighteenth century, it was a small but thriving port where cargo – notably cotton, rum and tobacco from the West Indies – destined for Lancaster, was unloaded. References in numerous guide books to Sunderland Point's 'cotton tree' having originated from 'a discarded cotton bale', are, alas, not true, for cotton comes from a shrub, not a tree, which grows only in the tropics. The tree in question is, in fact, a poplar which produces so many fluffy white seeds that they can completely cover the ground and often resemble a carpet of snow.

Near the end of the road at Sunderland Point, some of the life on the muddy flats can be seen by walking carefully over the bare banks. In the summer of 1982 I found much evidence of the previous severe winter, for everywhere I looked, pairs of large gaper shells, rarely seen above the surface when alive, were projecting out of the mud. Sure enough, when I pulled out a pair of gapers, the insides had been replaced by mud and the shells were blackened from bacteria producing a potent smell of bad eggs. Many cockle shells were scattered over the mud. These, too, had been killed as a result of persistently low air temperatures when the mud was exposed by the ebbing tide.

Some of the animals which live in the open water – such as jellyfish and comb jellies – inevitably get channelled into the estuary and later beached on the mud. At Sunderland Point, I spotted a stranded compass jellyfish which can be recognised by distinct brown radiating lines on the upper bell.

Brown seaweeds which blanket sheltered rocky shores are only able to grow in estuaries where they can attach themselves to pier supports, a buoy or derelict boats. Even then, they never grow so luxuriantly as on the open coast where the water is much less turbid and so allows sunlight to penetrate to a greater depth. I noticed that seaweeds had taken advantage of a mooring rope at Sunderland Point and were growing along its entire length.

From April to August, Sunderland fishermen can be seen wading out into the estuary to catch salmon in their huge hand-held haaf nets. Like eels, salmon migrate back and forth through estuaries to their feeding and breeding grounds. After hatching out as alevins in fresh water, salmon pass through the fingerling, parr and smolt stages before they migrate out to sea to feed for several years around the Greenland

At the stage when elvers reach river mouths after their long transatlantic migration, they are still so transparent that their backbones are clearly visible.

coastline, returning up estuaries to breed in rivers. Eels, on the other hand, hatch out in the open ocean (in the Sargasso Sea area). They migrate first as leaf-like Leptocephalus larvae which bear little resemblance to the adult eels. These change into elvers and then migrate up an estuary to feed in a river for several years before returning downriver to the sea.

With the exception of enthusiastic birdwatchers, few people are attracted to estuaries. They are easily the least popular of all our coastal habitats rating a poor third to sandy beaches and rocky shores. Yet for me, estuaries hold a special fascination. It is the element of un-certainty, of not knowing quite what I may come across, which attracts me to these desolate muddy expanses. Unfortunately their apparent emptiness and plentiful water supply have also attracted industry and power stations. More developments are planned – oil terminals and tidal barrages – both of which are likely to affect estuarine wildlife, notably birds. We know that oil spills always leave their toll of dead birds, but the effects of an estuarine tidal barrage are much more difficult to predict, particularly in areas that man has, until now, largely avoided.

NEW LIFE
ON AN OLD RAILWAY

Over little more than half a century, the coming of the railways to Britain reshaped the landscape. Since tracks could only be laid on level ground which was relatively straight, cuttings were excavated, embankments created, tunnels dug, and bridges and viaducts built. During the height of the railway creation some twenty tons of earth were shifted each day by navvies – the men who toiled to clear the routes and lay the tracks.

When George Stephenson opened the Stockton and Darlington Railway in 1825, it was the first route in the world to carry passengers, and from the end of the last century to the early part of this one the railways were in their heyday. When they were nationalised in 1948, British Rail took over some 30,600 kilometres (19,000 miles) of track. Between 1952 and 1967 – thanks mainly to Dr Beeching's 1963 report – massive closures of unprofitable branch lines were made, so that the working rail system was almost halved to a mere 17,700 kilometres (11,000 miles). But British Rail's loss of so many lines has been a positive gain to anyone who enjoys exploring the countryside or investigating past history on foot or by cycling. Wherever you live in Britain, there will be a disused railway somewhere close at hand. They can be found on detailed Ordnance Survey maps, or on a single map produced by HMSO in 1982 which

A line of bricks is all that remains of the old station in Haskayne cutting, now overgrown with grasses and a profusion of wild flowers.

shows the disused railways, existing railway paths and potential cycle routes along old railway routes in England and Wales.

Although the lines that are still operational are kept weed-free by regular spraying of herbicides, a wide range of wild flowers grow on railway cuttings and embankments up and down the country. As in any habitat, the type of soil, the extent of the drainage and the aspect all influence which plants are most likely to flourish. During train journeys throughout the country, I have seen dense bands of butterbur along damp stretches, ox-eye daisies and even wild orchids pushing up on south-facing chalk banks, primroses and violets flourishing where scrub has been cut down, and rosebay willowherb invading burnt ground.

When railway tracks are first abandoned, the track-sides and clinker beds are rapidly colonised by the seeds of annual plants (those that flower and die within a year) growing on adjacent banks. Sticky groundsel, wallcress, whitlow grass and corn salad, are all quick to take the opportunity to spread over well-drained waste ground. Oxford ragwort is another plant which now thrives on railway lines. After the yellow daisy-like flowers fade, copious wind-borne seeds are produced, and when their miniature parachutes open they are carried away by air currents. Originally introduced to Britain in 1699 in the Oxford Botanic Gardens, the plant took a century to spread out on to the Oxford walls and almost another century to reach the Great Western Railway

*Trains criss-crossing the country have spread the
wind-blown seeds of the Oxford ragwort, making the
plant a common feature of the railway landscape.*

track in 1877. Once there, however, it spread
quickly, for the clinker ash closely resembled its
home on the volcanic deposits of Mount Etna in
Sicily. The spread of Oxford ragwort was greatly
accelerated along this line by seeds blowing
into the open carriage windows and out again,
travelling via Reading, Swindon, Bristol and
Cardiff to Cardigan. The plant now occurs over
most of England and Wales and in parts of
Scotland and Ireland, and thanks to the widespread use of clinkers, is more common in
England than anywhere else in the world.

Succeeding the annuals come the biennials
(plants which usually flower in their second
year), shrubs and trees, until ultimately woodland develops. After thirty years of invasion by
shrubs and trees, many lines are now totally

overgrown. But, in places, some stretches of
disused tracks have been 'cleaned up' by local
councils and converted into tracks for pedes-
trians and cyclists. Others are being managed
as local nature reserves, for many of the old
tracks are important wildlife refuges in otherwise urban, suburban or agricultural settings.
The very nature of the construction of railway
lines means that they are set apart from the
surrounding land; embankments raised above it
tend to be well-drained, dry habitats, while
cuttings are liable to be damp or maybe even
flooded.

The Wirral Way, which lies in Cheshire between the Mersey and the Dee estuaries, is an
example of what can be done with a 19-
kilometre (12-mile) stretch of disused line.
Opened in 1973, it was one of the first two
Country Parks to be declared in Britain, with its
own visitor centre. The cost of providing a dozen
rangers and running the park is some £100,000 a
year, but spread among the half million annual
visitors it is good value for money. Along 11
kilometres (7 miles) of the track there are
superb views of the Dee estuary where
thousands of waders congregate in winter.

Haskayne Cutting, in Lancashire, is run on a
more modest scale as a local nature reserve by
the Lancashire Trust for Nature Conservation.*
Most of the reserve, which is just over 3
kilometres (2 miles) long, runs through a narrow
cutting, but in one place the level ground
broadens out considerably. This is the site of an
old siding and a signal box at Altcar and
Hillhouse station. Surrounded by agricultural
land, the reserve is a haven for wildlife, which is
surprisingly varied along different stretches of
the line, that includes dry embankments, bare
rock, rough grassland, marshy ground, foot-
paths and ditches.

*A permit is required to visit this reserve and can be
obtained from the reserve manager: Mrs Barbara Yorke,
3 Wicks Lane, Formby, Merseyside L37 3JE.

The cutting was created as part of the Downholland Branch Line of the Liverpool, Southport and Preston Junction Railway. The line was opened in 1887, but by July 1906 when the Altcar Bob – a steam railmotor – made its debut, it had become part of the larger Lancashire and Yorkshire Railway Company. The advantage of the Altcar Bob – a tiny tank engine with a single coach attached – was that when it wanted to change direction, it simply reversed like a tramcar, thus quickly nipping along the line between the halts. Once darkness fell at Plex Moss Lane Halt, where there was no platform, passengers had to resort to striking a match to catch the driver's attention. A bonus for the crew was the game rota they ran for any pheasants which were accidentally hit when they strayed across the line.

As well as carrying passengers, the line enabled farmers to get their fresh vegetables quickly despatched to Liverpool and Southport markets. But the coming of the motor car drastically cut the existing small nucleus of passengers, so that in 1938 this service was disbanded and the branch line was finally closed in 1952.

In 1953–4 the track was lifted, the station demolished and the signals removed. Then the wild flowers and scrub began to invade the old railway. Willows, with their wind-borne seeds, are particularly quick to spread, but in the drier parts silver birches take over, while alders thrive in waterlogged ground. The upper surfaces of many of the alder leaves are often covered in yellowish wart-like growths. These pouch galls are induced by parasitic mites living inside the leaves. As the galls age, they change colour to orange, then purple and finally reddish brown.

Most of the wild flowers grow best out in the open away from the shade of trees. In midsummer, the old station area is a blaze of colour, surrounded by large areas of rosebay willowherb, and smaller patches of blue sca-

A mating pair of recently emerged five-spot burnet moths rests on a rosebay willowherb flower.

bious, purple knapweed, cream meadow sweet, yellow loosestrife and St John's wort.

Now that so much of our summer landscape up and down the country is enlivened by the huge swards of pink rosebay willowherb spikes, which can be seen from a mile or more away, it is difficult to believe a century ago it was a relatively local wild plant in Britain. Known also as fireweed and cultivated in gardens in Elizabethan times, this plant quickly spreads over burnt ground. It flourished in London bomb sites after the Second World War, and has now spread all over Britain via forest fires and burnt embankments as well as waste ground and felled woodland. Like Oxford ragwort, it produces hairy seeds which are dispersed by the wind. From just one plant some 80,000 seeds are produced, hence the rapid spread of this attractive plant. Also, since there are so many individual flowers on the large flower spike, the

Dwarfed by a thistle seed, a meadow grasshopper 'sings' by rubbing its hind legs together, in an attempt to attract a possible mate.

lower ones are dispersing their seeds before the uppermost buds are even open. This means that seed from a single plant can be produced over a two month period, during which time the wind direction will change, so the seeds disperse in all directions.

The soil in Haskayne cutting is generally sandy and several of the plants, such as kidney vetch, common centaury and creeping willow, are typical of coastal sand dunes. Lying on the ground are the sections of a sandstone core removed by the North-West Water Authority when they bored an artesian well on the site, and on a sunny day lizards enjoy basking on the warm bare stone.

Insects also abound in the cutting. Late in July, I counted dozens of small tortoiseshells feeding on a clump of creeping thistles, yet I

could see only a few 5-spot burnet moths – all with battered almost scaleless wings – when a fortnight earlier hundreds were emerging from their cocoons. Maybe they could not withstand the prolonged heavy storm which had flooded nearby areas a few days previously. On warm days grasshoppers can be heard calling, each kind producing its own distinctive 'song' by rubbing a leg against part of the wing so that it sets up vibrations. With practice, it is possible to accurately identify grasshoppers (and crickets) by their individual songs; indeed, like radio commentators they are better known by their sound than by their shape, since grasshoppers are cryptically coloured to blend in with the surrounding vegetation.

The amazing variety of this reserve is not produced simply by leaving it all to nature. A great deal of work has to be done to maintain areas in which short-stemmed plants, notably wild orchids, will flourish. This means that the grass needs to be burnt or cut annually, and willow scrub kept in check, especially in the narrow stretches of the cutting, where it soon casts a heavy shade on the floor itself. By contrast, the middle section of the reserve has been intentionally left overgrown so as to provide cover and nesting sites for birds. In early autumn, flocks of linnets and redpolls roost in the cutting, and roving bands of tits pass through, while later in autumn fieldfares and redwings invade. At any time of year, thrushes seek out snails to feed on and I noticed the birds had used both the old platforms and an old sleeper as anvils where they had cracked open the shells to get at the flesh inside.

On the embankments beside the station there are remnants of cultivated plants which once grew in the station garden – plants such as ox-eye daisies, goldenrod and garden strawberries. Maybe the latter originated from a box destined for market which dropped off the train.

When shrubs and saplings grow up in old cuttings, they provide ideal song-posts for birds.

Compared with most churchyards, railway tracks are relatively recent habitats for wildlife. But, over the decades, generations of plants and animals have taken over cuttings and embankments, where they can live free of too much human interference. When the lines have been lifted, the wildlife is ready to move in; frogs and toads spawn in the water-filled ditches, and foxes, badgers and even deer use these traffic-free corridors to travel quickly across the countryside. At a time when more and more land is being used for building and farming, the old railway tracks are one area where wildlife is on the advance rather than at the retreat.

THE 'BEASTS OF THE FOREST'

Before wild boars became extinct in Britain in the early seventeenth century, they were known, together with fallow deer, red deer and, until the fourteenth century, roe deer, as 'beasts of the forest', and as such they belonged to the monarch. The roe deer was not favoured as a beast of the chase since it would not keep running for any great distance like the fallow and red deer, and so was not considered such good sport. The right to hunt these animals was a privilege which royalty jealously guarded, and large tracts of land were set aside as royal hunting preserves. One of the largest of these, the New Forest in Hampshire, was created by William I in 1079. Royal permission had to be gained by noblemen who wished to create hunting chases, or tracts of unenclosed land on their own estates, and examples of these may still be seen today at Cannock Chase in Staffordshire and Cranborne Chase in Dorset.

Enclosed deer parks were a later innovation, created mainly in the thirteenth and fourteenth centuries by the gentry to ensure a ready supply of venison during the harsh winter months. Even these required a costly licence from the Crown. The deer were contained by a ditch bordered by a bank, itself often topped with a hedge or a wall, since fallow deer in particular are very athletic. Places where an old hedgerow runs along an earthen bank are very likely to mark the location of old deer park boundaries. Once in captivity, the deer were ceremonially hunted with packs of buckhounds, which are slightly larger than foxhounds. There are still four deer-hunting packs in existence in England. The Devon and Somerset, Tiverton and Quantock deerhounds centre their activities on the red deer stags and hinds on Exmoor, while the New Forest Buckhound Pack is the only one concentrating on fallow deer and, since the First World War, it has been restricted to fallow bucks. In contrast to the red hunting jackets of the foxhound officials, the men who hunt with the New Forest buckhounds wear green. Apart from these packs, one of the few reminders of the former importance of deer hunting are the Ascot Races, which were founded in 1711 for the horses which hunted with the Royal Buckhounds in Richmond Park, and one of the races is still known today as the Royal Hunt Cup.

As the parks became increasingly expensive to maintain, many fell into disrepair and the land was developed for agriculture. By the eighteenth century, parks created by rich noblemen became predominantly ornamental. They were often imaginatively landscaped to create attractive vistas and glades in which deer grazed peacefully since, by then, fox-hunting had become a more popular sport. During the present century, many more parks have reverted to farmland although some still survive intact and are used for education or recreation.

In the heart of England, 10 kilometres (6 miles) from Leicester, lies Bradgate Park, which was one of nine areas of parkland surrounding the ancient forest of Charnwood. In 1241 Bradgate's deer were enclosed by ditches, hedges and oak palings for hunting. Hunting

The distorted shapes of stag-headed oak trees, many hundreds of years old, loom up out of the mist on an autumn morning in Bradgate Park.

and hawking were not only popular sports in medieval times, but also a very important means of obtaining food. Deer were then hunted with hounds and brought down with bows and arrows.

Bradgate House, now ruined, was one of the earliest unfortified great houses in Britain built entirely for pleasure. Begun by Thomas Grey in 1490, the E-shaped, brick Tudor house was finished by his son, grandfather of the nine-day Queen, Lady Jane Grey. In 1924, Mrs Katherine Grey sold Bradgate to Charles Bennion, a local industrialist. He in turn donated it to the City and County of Leicester, on the condition that it remained an open space where the wildlife would be preserved and the public could have free access. Since then, much of the 400-hectare

Dead bracken fronds complement the mellow brick ruins of Bradgate House.

(1,000-acre) park has been opened to the public, although the Deer Sanctuary, where the deer can rear their young safely, is kept undisturbed. There are now about 300 head of deer – 170 fallow and 130 red – which roam freely through the park, contained within stone walls which were built in the middle of the last century to replace the earlier oak paling. Two of the original deer-leaps – earth ramps leading up to the outside wall – have been retained in the perimeter wall. These leaps had a dual purpose: to encourage wild deer into the park, and to allow errant deer to return, by walking up the ramp and jumping down inside the wall.

Fallow deer became extinct in Britain during the last Ice Age, but they were probably introduced from Europe in the Middle Ages and today are the deer most often kept in parks. They are now also the most widely distributed of all the species of deer which live wild in Britain, no doubt because many of them escaped from derelict parks. Most fallow deer sport a brown summer coat with white spots and a black stripe running along the length of the backbone, giving them a beautiful dappled appearance. In winter, the coat darkens and the spots disappear. Fallow also exist in white and dark chocolate 'black' varieties. A herd of 200 head of white fallow lives in Houghton Park, Norfolk, where all other coloured individuals have been selectively culled. Their normally coloured eyes show that they are not albinos, whose pink eyes lack pigment. All of the wild fallow deer in Epping Forest – originally part of a huge hunting preserve known as Waltham Forest – used to be the 'black' variety but browns have been on the increase since 1953 when the first one was sighted.

During the autumnal rut, the deep throaty call of the male buck can be heard from afar. He constantly patrols his territory, periodically thrashing at scrub and bracken with his antlers, and scraping the ground with his hooves, to

Spotlit in a shaft of early morning sunlight, a fallow buck calls beside one of his does.

round up his does and ward off intruding bucks, although fallow bucks are not nearly so intent at fighting one another as are the red stags. The peak of the rut occurs during the last two weeks in October when the buck mates with the does, each of whom usually gives birth to a single fawn eight months later in mid-June.

Only the male deer develop antlers. These start growing out from the skull of a young fawn as small bony knobs in the first winter, when it is about six months old. Growing antlers are covered with a fine, furry skin known as 'velvet' which dies and is shed at the end of summer. In August, fallow bucks can often be seen with the velvet hanging down in strips from their antlers, and at this stage they frequently rub their antlers against trees or other hard objects to remove the velvety skin. Fallow bucks cast their antlers in the following spring, after which a new pair begins growing immediately. During the early years of the buck's life, each new pair of antlers is larger than the cast pair, until ultimately the characteristic palm-shaped antlers develop. Fallow deer feed on a wide variety of food, grazing on grass and browsing on trees, and in the autumn feasting themselves on acorns, chestnuts, beech mast and even on occasional fungi.

Red and roe deer are both native to Britain. In the wild, red deer – the largest of the British species – have their stronghold on the moors of Scotland, although originally they were animals of woodland. For a number of years, the red deer on the Hebridean island of Rhum – itself a nature reserve – have been studied to see how they behave and breed, and coloured collars and ear tags have enabled biologists to follow individual animals throughout the seasons.

In winter, the red deer's reddish-brown summer coat, turns a dark brown or a grey-brown. During the autumnal rut, which falls earlier than the fallow rut, peaking at the end of September to mid-October, the stag utters his magnificent roar and wallows even more frequently in muddy hollows. As the mud dries, it cakes on to his coat, giving him a somewhat scruffy appearance. No other animal in Britain utters such a dramatic sound as a rutting red stag – especially when heard in the wilds of Scotland If his territory is challenged by another stag who has not been intimidated by the roar, he turns broadside, and if this is still of no avail, the two stags may meet each other head-on with crashing antlers. Young red deer, which are known as calves, are born at the end of May or early in June. Like fallow fawns, they have a dappled coat which helps to camouflage them amongst the vegetation.

Unlike Britain's wild deer, parkland animals can be seen quite easily at any time of day, but it is well worth getting up at dawn to see the

During the autumn rut, a red deer stag defends his territory with a bellowing roar.

fallow bucks and the red stags during their rut. Not only will the deer be more active at this time of day, but also the misty atmosphere of the autumnal mornings is soon lost once the sun breaks through.

Of the deer parks still surviving, the best known are probably Woburn in Bedfordshire, Richmond in Surrey, Petworth in Sussex and

These red deer hinds are on the alert and ready to move as soon as they sense an intruder.

Chatsworth in Derbyshire. Woburn, which is most famed as being Britain's first safari park, has been the home of the Dukes of Bedford for over 300 years. The deer park was landscaped by Humphrey Repton in the early part of the nineteenth century, and it was the eleventh Duke of Bedford who brought the original herd of the very rare Père David deer to Woburn around the turn of the century, by buying them from various European zoos. Descendants of a captive herd in the Chinese Imperial Hunting

Park near Peking, these deer were only saved from extinction by successful breeding at Woburn. The current world population of about 550 deer are all descended from the original Woburn herd. In more recent years, several kinds of deer have been introduced to the 1,200-hectare (3,000-acre) park, and there are currently eight other species at Woburn – red, fallow, axis, rusa, Manchurian sika, barasingha, muntjac and Chinese water deer.

Richmond Park, now surrounded by London's suburbs, was created and enclosed as a royal hunting ground in the reign of Charles I. Some 600 head of deer – both fallow and red – can be seen quite easily when walking or driving through the Park. During the mating season however, when the fallow bucks and red stags are defending their territories with their does and hinds respectively, it is wise to keep a safe distance away.

The grounds of both Chatsworth and Petworth were landscaped by Capability Brown. The 270-hectare (670-acre) deer park at Petworth was enclosed by a 21-kilometre (13-mile) long stone wall in 1750. Its herd of fallow deer is the largest enclosed one in Europe, numbering 1,200 head in summer and being culled down to 800 head in winter. Roe, red and muntjac are also kept in Petworth Park. The roe herd is quite unsurpassed for quality. Recent skull measurements suggest that this herd is unique and may well stem from stock dating back to Roman times. This species, the smallest of the British deer, is quite secretive in the wild and it does not readily adjust to parkland conditions, so it is not often enclosed today.

Other parkland deer have become used to the presence of humans so their behaviour can be observed at close quarters without spending a great deal of time and effort trying to stalk them and to outwit their acute sense of smell. For the purist, there is nothing to compare with stalking deer in the wild, but many people none the less gain a great deal of pleasure watching deer in a park, coupled with much excitement at being an onlooker during the rutting season.

Deer parks have much more to offer than deer alone, and often they have fine examples of trees that have been able to grow in the open for hundreds of years. Specimen oaks, in particular, can grow to impressive proportions. In Bradgate, however, many of the distorted solitary oak trees are decaying. Their bizarre shapes have been created by the ancient practice of pollarding whereby the tops of the trunks were lopped some 2·5–3·5 metres (8–12 feet) from the ground in a 15-year rotation to provide fuel for the tenants. Oak twigs were also cut and given to the deer as winter food.

At the end of the fifteenth century, sweet chestnut and hazel were planted in Bradgate for coppicing to provide charcoal or wood for fuel. Coppiced trees can always be recognised by their multiple slender trunks sprouting up from ground level, where the tree is cut down every decade or so. When shooting was a popular sport in the Park, hollow oak trees were used by pheasant poachers for stowing away their haul which they doped by baiting the birds with currants soaked in whisky!

Bradgate Park is the only medieval deer park in Leicestershire where the original landscape remains virtually intact. Like most other surviving deer parks, Bradgate's function has now changed completely. Initially cleared and enclosed to keep intruders out, it is now deliberately maintained to attract visitors, and every year a million of them come to enjoy its natural beauty. As visitors stroll through the woodlands, spinneys and bracken-covered hills dotted with granite outcrops, they can appreciate the deer as well as all the other associated animals and plants, while a climb up to the high tops provides a magnificent panoramic view.

A TWENTIETH-CENTURY HAVEN

Few people, as they hurtle up and down the A1 trunk road past Ferrybridge in Yorkshire, would appreciate that they are within a stone's-throw of a unique nature reserve. Overshadowed by Ferrybridge power station, Fairburn Ings comprises extensive areas of open water, as well as marshland, drainage ditches, spoil tips and low-lying farmland. Fairburn Ings is owned by the National Coal Board and now managed by the Royal Society for the Protection of Birds, and as a result of much voluntary work, large numbers of waterfowl can be seen from the village road and viewed from even closer quarters inside hides overlooking the water. In a small way, this comparatively new site helps to redress the balance of wetlands which has been lost elsewhere in Britain through land drainage.

Accounts of this marshy ground beside the River Aire between Ferrybridge and Castleford go back as far as the seventh century when Penda, King of Mercia, was killed in the Battle of Winwood in 655. His men fled to the south until they reached the Aire at Ferrybridge where many were drowned in the flooded marshes. In 1069, William the Conqueror was held up for three weeks in this area when the nearby Brotherton Marsh was temporarily under water. The name Fairburn has evolved from the Saxon name Farenburne (the stream among the ferns) and Fareburn as it is recorded in the Domesday Book. By the seventeenth century, the marshes

Waterfowl have quickly taken advantage of the flooded farmland at Fairburn Ings.

between Fairburn and the neighouring village of Newton had been drained so that they could be farmed, but they were still subject to flooding when the river overflowed its banks. 'Ings' is a Viking word used to describe seasonally flooded water meadows and was therefore a more appropriate name in the past than today, when much of the area is now permanently flooded.

During the last century coal mining began in the area, but it was not until the early part of this century that the land began to subside, resulting in the large areas of open water which can be seen at Fairburn today.

Records of game and wildfowl shot on the Fairburn estate during 1899–1900 prove that the terrain was much drier than it is today, since in 40 days shooting 138 brace of partridge, 67 couples of rabbit and only a single coot were taken. At this time, shallow temporary water attracted surface-feeding or dabbling ducks such as mallard, teal and wigeon, whereas now diving ducks like tufted duck and pochard, as well as coots, are much in evidence, feeding on submerged aquatic plants which can flourish in the permanent water. When Nelson's *Birds of Yorkshire* was published in 1907 he made no reference to Fairburn, and it was not until the First World War that the ornithological significance of this site began to be appreciated.

Each year the area of open water increases as the surrounding farmland gradually submerges, and the farmers' loss becomes nature's gain. The boundaries of fields which were flooded in the late 1970s can still be traced by the line of stark, dead hawthorns and the tops of the fence posts. In 1982, I noticed a clump of bulrushes flourishing quite incongruously amidst an expanse of barley stubble, further proof of subsidence under way.

Wildfowl and waders are quick to take advantage of new expanses of water, and the 80 hectares (200 acres) of permanent open water at Fairburn now attract a wide variety of these and other birds. Ornithologists have logged in over 240 species at Fairburn, which is situated next to a migration route through the Pennines

Almost a third of these species have stayed long enough to breed. As well as the more common waterfowl such as mallard, teal, tufted

In severe weather, tufted duck keep a small patch of water free of ice by constantly swimming.

duck, coots and moorhens, breeding birds have included Canada geese, snipe, great crested and little grebes and, in 1982, the first pair of common terns.

Each season brings a change of visitors. At the end of the summer after the spring influx of birds arriving to breed, huge flocks of sand martins and swallows congregate prior to their migration to warmer winter resorts. Ducks and other water birds use Fairburn as a winter refuge. The numbers are prodigious; on average there are 1,000 mallard, 500 teal, 400 tufted duck and 500 coots, as well as 30–50 whooper swans that fly down from Scandinavia and Russia to benefit from Yorkshire's comparatively mild climate.

Detailed records of the numbers of birds visiting Fairburn show in many cases a gradual,

but spectacular, build-up over the years. Gadwall, for example, never very common in Britain, were unknown in the area in 1953, but are now present in most months, with a maximum count of 67 in 1974. Numbers of visiting Canada geese have fluctuated greatly. Six birds with their wings clipped were released at Fairburn in July 1966, in the hope that they would attract wild birds to join them, and the geese did indeed breed successfully in the following year. In 1982, 21 breeding pairs were joined by more geese in late June to make a total of 219 birds. The large size of the geese make them easy to pick out when they are swimming or feeding on land, and late in summer they can be seen flying off at dusk to feed in nearby stubble fields.

Even in the best managed reserves, some species decline where others increase. Mute swans first appeared at Fairburn at the turn of the century. Although present throughout the year, most can be seen in the summer between July and September when the submerged plants – Canadian pondweed, water crowfoot and fennel pondweed – on which they feed, are growing vigorously. In August 1960, 216 mute swans were recorded, but in 1982 there were 11 nesting pairs and only 6 of these bore young. In the summer of 1910 some 50 black-headed gulls arrived and in 1912 large numbers of eggs were found on the natural islands – the remnants of the high ground. Eventually as many as 250–300 pairs bred annually, but mining subsidence and fluctuating water levels reduced the number of potential breeding sites (typically a scrape in the ground, or built up on accumulated plants) and the size of the colony. Then in 1980, two floating rafts were introduced to the reserve as nesting sites for these gulls, and four pairs of gulls nested on the rafts in that year. A year later, 24 pairs nested on four rafts and in 1982 65 pairs nested on six rafts. Each raft is made from a pair of telegraph poles, joined together by wires so the poles are a metre (three feet)

apart. The area between the poles is then filled with sweet grass, bulrushes and yellow flag which soon begin to sprout anew. The advantage of floating nest sites is that they move up and down as the water level rises and falls and so do not flood. The declining trend of the breeding gulls has been successfully reversed and in spring and autumn, huge roosts of these birds can be seen congregating at Fairburn, the record being 22,000 on one night in March 1965.

A reserve like Fairburn needs careful management to ensure that there is sufficient range of habitats for a variety of species. The few areas of bare mud, which are so attractive to waders, are very vulnerable to rising water levels, so the shortage of bare mud for nest scrapes is a recurring problem. Buttonweed, an introduced plant which produces flat button-like heads, was first recorded in 1962 and has spread rapidly over the mud. In late summer, when seen from a distance, these plants resemble a field of buttercups, adding a welcome splash of colour to the marshy surrounds. However,

Originally brought into Britain as an ornamental wetland bird in the seventeenth century, the Canada goose has since become well established in the wild.

buttonweed and celery-leaved crowfoot are both so effective at colonising bare muddy patches, that they too are contributing to the loss of the waders' already restricted habitat.

Fairburn is a focal point which attracts many migrating birds *en route* to and from their breeding grounds as they fly along the Aire Valley passing through the Pennines via the 'Aire Gap'. Many are predictable visitors which return each year, while others are rarities which turn up when freak weather conditions occur. During the spring, birds which overwinter south of Britain drop in on Fairburn to feed before continuing to fly northwards to their breeding grounds. In the summer, large numbers of swallows and sand martins converge on Fairburn to gorge themselves on the big hatches of midges emerging from the water, before flying south to Africa. Towards mid-September during the period 1959–1965 more than a million birds roosted at night in the reed beds at Fairburn. What a spectacle all these birds must have been, silhouetted against the setting sun, as they wove their way across the sky. As swallows and sand martins begin to take up their positions in a roost, they start twittering, until eventually the sound of so many birds becomes quite deafening. Suddenly, all noise ceases and, by comparison, the air is abnormally quiet.

Rare birds which have appeared at Fairburn include the red-necked grebe, Slavonian grebe, Leach's petrel, velvet scoter, grey phalarope and the Iceland gull. Spoonbills, which breed across the North Sea in the Netherlands and Denmark, have turned up in spring and summer after east winds have been blowing.

Considering the distance which many birds have to cover to reach Fairburn, it is not surprising that some unusual plants appear in the reserve. Although many plants originate from wind-blown seeds, others are transported as seeds on the feet of birds or maybe even pass out in their droppings.

A spectacular plant which graces Fairburn for several months in the summer is Himalayan balsam. Reaching up to 2 metres (6 feet) tall, it was introduced to Britain in 1839 and grown in greenhouses. When gardeners realised that the succulent stems belied the robustness of this annual plant, they put it outside in borders. From here, it escaped via streams to rivers and other waterways, greatly accelerated by its buoyant seeds. The green seed capsules which develop after the large pink flowers fade, violently explode when ripe, separating into five parts, each of which suddenly rolls up, catapulting its seeds in all directions. Once seen, few people can resist the temptation of speeding the dispersal by gently touching the capsules which immediately burst open.

At first, the early plant colonisers at Fairburn spread rapidly to form extensive areas of a single species, but gradually other plants have begun to move in and now the reserve supports a variety of plants, both above and below water level, which provides abundant food for the wildfowl. Dabbling ducks consume large numbers of seeds, and during the winter at Fairburn they feed chiefly on fennel pondweed, marestail and reed sweet-grass. Diving ducks such as tufted duck and goldeneye frequent extensive beds of fennel pondweed and water-milfoil where they not only feed on the seeds, but also on the large numbers of aquatic organisms which live among the finely divided branches. If waterfowl are to breed, however, there must be some sort of cover to which the adults can retreat and where the nest and the young are protected from prevailing winds and predators. At Fairburn, large stands of bulrushes and reed sweet-grass serve this purpose.

Spoil tips, a legacy of the mining that created this haven for birds, present problems for plants in the area. Some of the original species have not been able to cope with the changes that mining has brought with it. The water violet, for

example, which actually belongs to the primrose family, has completely disappeared from
the nearby Newton Ings. Bare spoil tips erode
rapidly and the water which runs off them is
laden with silt which has a high concentration
of minerals and also smothers plants. However,
old tips in the reserve, which are no longer in
use, have been planted with a variety of trees,
which prevent erosion of the spoil and provide
cover and food for terrestrial birds. It is quite
surprising to find how many trees and wild
flowers can grow on the spoil tips, as a walk
along the path beside the River Aire will reveal.
The waste which the colliery now produces is in
a liquid suspension and is piped into lagoons
outside the reserve where it settles out, so the
problem of spoil has been reduced.

The Ings serve as washlands for neighbouring
Castleford, receiving the rainwater run-off during periods of heavy rain at any time of year –
but especially in winter. This brings about a rise
in the water level at Fairburn. The Ings drain
into the Aire via a man-made channel, and the
removal of excess water can be accelerated by
winding up the sluice gates. In severe weather,
the Ings freeze over almost completely, apart
from small patches of water in the centre which
are kept open by birds as they move around in
search of food.

No one who drives along the road bordering
the northern edge of Fairburn Ings can fail to
notice the feeding station on the Newton road.
Every day in winter or summer, people walk out
on to the peninsula, provided by the local
authority, to feed the birds. This honeypot area
does provide an opportunity to see mute swans,
Canada geese and coots at close range,
although it does not provide a feel of Fairburn
Ings as a whole.

Maintaining a thriving reserve is hard work.
As well as the introduction of floating nest rafts,
the tasks involve the excavation of bare mud,
the coppicing of willows to provide shrubby

*Mute swans, here seen with their young, Canada geese
and tufted duck are some of the waterfowl which can be
seen all the year round at Fairburn.*

growth as nesting sites for reed warblers, the
removal of encroaching sycamores, as well as
the erection and repair of hides for visitors'
enjoyment.

Looking after a reserve which is constantly
changing inevitably brings problems, but it is
for precisely this reason that you can never be
certain when new plants and animals will
appear, making Fairburn an especially interesting place to visit – at any time of year.

WILDLIFE IN THE GARDEN

For a gardener who aims to produce perfect prize-winning flowers and vegetables, the intrusion of wildlife in the form of pests and predators is something to be avoided at all costs. But anyone who enjoys wildlife can create their own miniature nature reserve within their garden simply by not keeping it too neat and tidy. A garden with a mosaic of habitats – a pond, old stone walling, a compost heap, a pile of old logs, a bramble patch, berried trees and shrubs – will attract and harbour much richer wildlife than one with a neat lawn and weed-free borders. Blue tits and ladybirds can be far more effective at controlling pests than a squirt of insecticide, as well as being a good deal cheaper, safer and much less effort. Even a patch of stinging nettles is worth preserving; they are the food of the caterpillars of small tortoiseshell and peacock butterflies which when they hatch out, add a dynamic splash of colour to the herbaceous border.

The garden which I explored for the television series, abounds with wildlife. Looking out of a window one morning I spotted a robin and a blackbird feeding on the lawn, birds which you might find in any garden, but here they were only two out of a total of 48 species sighted over the last three years. During the winter, the birds are attracted to the well-stocked bird table, but once natural food becomes available, they are no longer fed. The table is sited outside the backdoor, within view of the kitchen window, but away from the sort of cover a hunting cat might use to stalk and pounce upon unwary birds. Squirrels are a nuisance at bird tables because they are very adept at stealing the food.

This can be controlled to some extent by placing plastic tubing around the supports of the table, which prevents them from getting a firm grip as they attempt to climb upwards. Beside the bird table is the other great attraction, an old weathered quern that functions as a bird bath. Seeing a family of starlings indulging in a group bath with the sunlight sparkling on the flying spray may be amusing for a while, but their presence unfortunately deters other birds from venturing into the bath.

The Yorkshire garden was created out of a woodland and many of the original trees have been left. These mature trees provide cover and nesting sites for the birds, and some dead trees – a legacy of a hurricane in 1962 – remain as nesting sites for woodpeckers. Additional nest sites can be provided in any garden by putting up nest boxes, which should be carefully positioned so that they are shaded and sheltered from the prevailing wind or direct sunlight. The size and shape of the boxes will determine what type of birds use them. Blue tits and great tits, for example, prefer to nest in boxes with small holes. In many localities, if the hole is not reinforced with a metal plate it will be enlarged by squirrels so they can attack the nestlings. Young birds may also sometimes fall prey to a great spotted woodpecker. The nest box will then be abandoned by the tits and may well be taken over by starlings. Robins and spotted flycatchers, on the other hand, prefer using open-fronted boxes.

The boggy edges of a garden pond are an attractive setting for native and introduced wetland plants.

A predatory ladybird larva climbs up a rose-bud for one of the many aphids it consumes daily.

Beside the lawn there is a small pond. Originally this was surrounded by stone paving, but now the paving is almost entirely camouflaged by a profusion of plants so that it blends in with the borders. Several species of water plants that are native to Britain, such as

bogbean and water soldier, have been introduced to the pond, and the boggy borders have been planted with royal ferns and attractive yellow-flowering primulas. Water soldier grows naturally in ponds, ditches and canals where the water is rich in lime. In the spring, the plants become buoyant and the funnel-shaped leaf rosettes float up and break the surface. The margins of all the leaves are armed with a sharp saw-like edge. The long roots which hang down from the base of the rosette stabilise the plants, and prevent them from turning over. Water soldier buds off small plants on the ends of runners so rapidly that only one plant need be introduced to a small pond and it will still soon choke out all other plants. White flowers are produced in summer, and after flowering the plants begin to sink as a chalky deposit builds up on the leaves. Fishermen do not welcome the introduction of water soldier into angling waters because not only do the spiny leaves snare their lines, but they also offer a safe haven to a multitude of small aquatic animals which would otherwise have fattened the fish. Duckweed is a much smaller plant but it too can be just as troublesome in ponds. The plants rapidly multiply by simply budding off more plants so that during warm weather the entire pond's surface becomes carpeted with duckweed. This cuts out much of the sunlight reaching the submerged plants below the surface, and prevents oxygenated water being mixed down to the bottom of the pond.

Water beetles, which are strong fliers, will make their own way to a new pond, although they sometimes come to grief when they mistake a moonlit greenhouse for a stretch of water. Dragonflies, too, can fly to a pond and lay their eggs.

A closer look at the water in the Yorkshire pond revealed pondskaters dashing around on the surface, using their long legs to spread the weight of their bodies which are prevented from sinking by the surface tension. Below the surface, I spotted water boatmen and water snails, and a dip with a net brought up some newt larvae still bearing their feathery gills. Apparently the goldfish went the way of many ornamental fish – down a heron's gullet. A layer of wire netting stretched over a pond will prevent herons from fishing, but it is rather unsightly. Another method of deterring herons from helping themselves to your fish is to erect a wire barrier around the pond margin which will prevent them from bending down to reach the water. They will also be unable to reach the fish if the pond sides are made vertical instead of sloping, but this makes it difficult for the small birds and mammals which visit the pond to drink, and to climb out safely unless a plank is provided. Alternatively, small birds will be able to drink by alighting on a short branch wedged into an upturned flowerpot in the pond itself.

The pond is a good place to get a close look at the structure of a water lily bloom. This flower shows clearly the way in which the outer petals protect the inner stamens, which produce the pollen, and stigmas on which the pollen grains must land for the flower to be pollinated. If plants are to produce seeds, they must be pollinated – either by their own pollen (self-pollination) or, as most often happens, by pollen from another flower (cross-pollination). Plants with large showy flowers like the water lily tend to be insect-pollinated, whereas plants with small yellow or greenish flowers such as grasses and many trees, are wind-pollinated.

Bees can often be seen foraging inside water lily flowers picking up pollen grains on their bodies as they move around. They are well worth attracting into gardens since they help to increase the yield of edible fruits by cross-pollination. Bees are attracted to plants which produce copious nectar and pollen, for they use nectar for making into honey, and pollen as a protein source for feeding to the larvae.

Bumble bees also squeeze into petunias and foxgloves, while smaller insects crawl over the flat umbrella-shaped flower-heads, or umbels, of plants of the carrot family. Flowers with long tubes such as hyacinth, tobacco and honey-

These ground beetles have crawled into the bottom of a stack of flowerpots after a night's hunting.

suckle are pollinated only by moths or butterflies which have tongues long enough to reach the nectar at the base of the tube. All these flowers produce a strong scent to lure pollinators; hyacinth by day, honeysuckle and tobacco by night. Honeysuckle buds open between 7 and 8 pm, emitting their strong scent well into the night, attracting hawk-moths and the silver-Y moth. Dame's violet or sweet rocket is another plant which releases a powerful perfume which wafts into the late evening air. It has a curious scent – a mixture of violets and cinnamon.

Many flowers have elaborate mechanisms which ensure that the insect visitor gets liberally dusted with pollen before it flies to another flower. In both snapdragon and bear's breeches the inner parts of the flowers are well protected by a hood and a lower platform. The relatively heavy weight of a bumble bee is needed to depress the landing platform so the insect can gain access to the innermost part of the flower where the nectar is produced. Some insects however – notably bumble bees – cheat deep-throated flowers by cutting a hole in the side of the flower so they can steal the nectar without struggling through the flower, brushing against the floral reproductive parts and pollinating it.

Butterflies can be enticed into the garden by growing some flowers which they seem to find irresistible. Buddleia, also known as the butterfly bush, never fails to attract butterflies – I have counted up to twenty butterflies of six species on a single bush. In September the flat heads of ice plants, packed with a mass of tiny flowers, as well as teasels and Michaelmas daisies, are popular with butterflies, which generally favour the simple cottage garden flowers in preference to showy garden cultivated varieties. When the last of the garden flowers are fading, butterflies will turn to ivy flowers or fallen rotting fruit. A bed of Michaelmas daisies will provide a later autumnal nectar top-up for hive bees before the winter frosts set in and they cease flying.

Many of our native wild flowers are also very attractive to butterflies and other insects, and centuries ago gardens were full of these flowers which were then cultivated for food or medicinal purposes. Nowadays it is illegal to uproot any wild plant from the British countryside without permission from the owner or the occupier, and 61 especially rare plants are completely protected by the 1981 Wildlife and Countryside Act. However, in recent years, several firms have begun marketing wild flower seeds, so that with careful attention and the correct soil type, it is possible to grow such plants as cowslip, foxglove, marsh mallow, meadowsweet, dark mullein, sea pea, poppy, rock rose, scabious, sweet cicely, teasel and woodruff in your own garden.

Maybe the prize-winning wild flower garden created for the 1982 Chelsea Flower Show will spark off a vogue for cultivating plants which, until quite recently, would have been classed as weeds. While some people may prefer to devote a corner of the garden to a wild flower sanctuary, many of these flowers can be intermingled very successfully with cultivated forms and introduced species.

In the autumn, birds feast themselves on seeds and fruits and berries. Fruits of bramble, elder, holly, ivy, barberry and rowan are all enjoyed by blackbirds, thrushes and later on by fieldfares and redwings, both winter visitors to Britain from Scandinavia and Siberia. But if you actively encourage birds into your garden you must not begrudge them the odd strawberry, raspberry or currant! You will also be lucky to retain holly berries up until Christmas, unless it is a particularly mild winter. If thistles and sunflowers are allowed to seed, they may well attract goldfinches.

Flowering currant is a shrub which bees find highly attractive and as they feed on its flowers so they help to pollinate them.

In contrast with birds, mammals that visit gardens are rarely seen because most are nocturnal. Many gardens harbour their resident bank voles and wood mice, but the only proof of their presence may be little tracks criss-crossing snow-covered ground. Deer may not be welcome in every garden as they will make short work of the rose bed, whereas hedgehogs should be encouraged because they will feed on slugs and snails. Hegehogs will readily drink milk from a saucer, and they can gradually be conditioned not to react to a torchlight. They often root around a compost heap in search of food, for a well-rotting heap will be crammed

Basking in the warmth of the sun, a red admiral feeds on a buddleia bush which was planted in the author's garden to attract butterflies.

with wildlife, beginning with microscopic bacteria which break down the cells of discarded plants, followed by worms, springtails, flies, mites, centipedes, woodlice, beetles, spiders, slugs and even snakes. The harmless grass-snake seeks warm places in which to lay its eggs, and so will often make use of the internal heat generated by a compost or a manure heap.

Now that hedgerows and ponds are fast dwindling from the countryside, gardens are becoming increasingly important as places where more and more wildlife can take refuge, feed and maybe even breed. The population explosion of the grey squirrel – an alien now officially classified in Britain as a pest – is much in evidence. Early in the morning you may catch sight of one frantically digging up your lawn to bury an acorn for its winter larder. Foxes are

A colourful clump of wood blewits, one of many species of fungus found in gardens, grows up through rotting leaves on a compost heap.

now frequent night-time raiders of dustbins in large cities such as London and Bristol, while blue tits have learned to take advantage of any foil-covered milk bottles left out on the doorstep. All gardeners delight in having a resident robin, but the persistent call of a collared dove, with its large appetite, from the top of a television aerial is a relatively new event that few people welcome.

A LUSH REEDSWAMP

Leighton Moss is one of Britain's most important reserves for wetland birds. It lies in a shallow valley which is flanked by low limestone ridges and opens out into the eastern side of Morecambe Bay. The valley was originally an inlet of the sea, and is lined with layers of clay laid down during that period. After the sea water receded, the poorly-drained clay flats became first a brackish swamp, then a reed swamp, and then they gradually formed an acid bog as *Sphagnum* moss moved in. For centuries the peaty hummocks dotted across the soggy ground of this raised bog prohibited a direct route around the perimeter of the bay. Peat cutting began around the edges of the bog, and the wet peat slabs were stacked up to dry before being used as fuel, as is still the practice today in parts of Scotland and Ireland. Patches of open water no doubt attracted wildfowl, since there are accounts of locals indulging in the sport of hunting wild duck – before they were able to fly – by using spaniels in nearby Carnforth Marsh.

In 1847, the land was reclaimed by pumping out the water to the sea through a system of dykes, initially by using a windmill, and then by a steam-operated pump. By the end of the nineteenth century nearly all the peat had been dug out. Once the Moss had been drained, it became rich arable land for root crops such as potatoes and turnips. The steam pump was powered by coal brought by train to nearby Silverdale Station until the supply of coal

While mallard congregate on the open water at Leighton Moss, a lone heron lurks in the background.

became short towards the end of the First World War. The pumping then stopped, so the Moss gradually filled up with the water which drained down from the surrounding hills and a shallow lake formed. Reeds began to spread out to the open water and, at a later stage, willows moved in forming willow 'carr' – the name for a woodland which develops on swampy ground.

This new wetland area attracted wildfowl, which in turn attracted wildfowlers. Bird records for the early part of the eighteenth century in the environs of Leighton indicate that not only were waders common at this time, but also the bittern, or bittour as it was known. Several breeding pairs of bitterns established themselves at Leighton Moss in the 1940s as these birds moved back to one of their traditional breeding haunts. The bitterns breed in the Moss's extensive and dense reedbeds – the most northern site where this kind of habitat, so characteristic of the Norfolk Broads, can be found.

By nature a highly secretive bird, the bittern when disturbed adopts an upright stance with the bill tip pointing skywards. This posture, together with the dappled plumage, makes the bittern difficult to spot among the reeds. Only when it emerges to feed in the open water at the edge of a reedbed or when the male 'booms' can it be located. The male utters his powerful and evocative booming call – not unlike a foghorn – from February to June.

Bitterns used to breed in England, Wales and Scotland, with their stronghold in the fenlands and broadlands of East Anglia. But wetland drainage drastically reduced their potential breeding sites, while shooting and egg-collecting also helped to accelerate the decline of these beautiful but shy birds. In 1868, the last nest with eggs was found in Norfolk, and after that the birds were seen no more. Then in 1900, bitterns were heard booming once again in the county. These were continental birds which had crossed the Channel to recolonise the area. Their numbers were gradually increased, although several birds died during the severe winters of 1946–47 and 1962–63. In recent years, the bittern has again declined in East Anglia and now a quarter of the country's breeding birds live at Leighton Moss. Because it is such a rare breeding bird in Britain it is completely protected by law.

Other birds of reedswamps, such as the reed warbler and the water rail, began to move in to breed at Leighton Moss in the 1920s. In 1964, the area became a reserve of the Royal Society for the Protection of Birds and, by extensive management, every vegetation stage in the natural succession from open water, through fen into woodland, is now present. Management is essential since the shallow open water areas, only 15–60 centimetres (6–24 inches) deep, would soon revert to solid reedbed and willow carr if left untouched.

Large areas of reeds are cleared by cutting them underwater, while small fringes at the water's edge are kept in check by spraying with herbicide. In winter, the green reeds turn to beige as they die back. Come the following spring, new growth sprouts up from the base, and as the temperature rises, all the shoots keep in step growing at a rate of 2·5 centimetres (1 inch) a day, forming a conspicuous green tide-line visibly advancing up the brownish backcloth.

To provide a favourable habitat for both breeding birds and insects, some of the willow scrub has been removed, while parts of it are now coppiced every five years. Reed warblers,

sedge warblers, reed buntings and wrens all nest in these coppiced willows, but it is the grasshopper warbler which is the star attraction. Its distinctive reeling song, which sounds more like an angler winding in a line than a singing grasshopper, is so high pitched that many older people are unable to hear it.

The eyed hawk moth caterpillar, which also lives in the willows, is one of the largest moth larvae which feeds on the leaves of these shrubby trees. It is very difficult to spot because it is so well camouflaged. Its green colour, coupled with diagonal lines, mimics a leaf complete with veins, and a subtle tonal gradation of the green completes the perfect disguise. When seen in the hand, the eyed hawk moth caterpillar clearly has a darker green underside. However, when the caterpillar rests, it clings upside down on a willow twig, and the combined effect of the light and the caterpillar's shading is that it appears the same tone of green all over. Because of this, it merges even better with the willow leaves. This uneven body colouration – known as counter-shading – is found throughout the natural world, and also occurs, for example, in mid-water fish such as mackerel.

Controlling the water level and the rate of flow is also an important part in successful reserve management. The dykes have to be kept cleared so that the flood level can be controlled with sluice gates and the water levels can be maintained. New islands have been created for breeding birds by dumping rocks and soil in shallow water areas and also by cutting away iris or yellow flag clumps, so they can be floated into position before being tethered to stakes.

Having read and heard many graphic accounts of the wildlife and the actual setting of Leighton Moss, I greatly looked forward to my

A reed warbler feeds craneflies to its young in a nest slung between swaying reeds.

Emerging from the water with a bedraggled coat, a water shrew adopts its characteristic pose with nose upturned to test the air.

first visit. I was not disappointed. Within minutes of entering a hide early on a May morning with the reserve warden, I heard and saw my first wild otter in Britain. As it surfaced, black-headed gulls mobbed it by swooping back and forth and the waterfowl swimming around the surface quickly moved off into the cover of the reeds. Otters are usually most active at night, but the peaceful surroundings at Leighton Moss tempt them out during the daytime. The times of otter sightings and their behaviour are recorded in books kept in the hides. It was here that I read an account by one keen naturalist who made the effort to rise at dawn and was rewarded at 4 a.m. by the sight of an otter swimming around chasing fish and finally succeeding in catching an eel before it swam off into the reeds. Eels form the main diet of the Leighton Moss otters, but they do also feed on other fish. Even though birds get very agitated when an otter surfaces, only rarely does a duck fall prey to this carnivore, which frequents the deeper pools or meres. Tracks in muddy and snow-covered ground prove they also move around on land.

Foxes, badgers, weasels, stoats and water voles may also be seen in the reserve, and I watched a water shrew nosing its way along the edge of a path for a full ten minutes before it disappeared into the undergrowth. Red squirrels live in the wooded margins of the Moss, while red deer are most likely to be seen in May when they move into the reedbeds to feed on the young reeds.

Besides the bittern, over 200 species of birds have been recorded at Leighton Moss, somewhat more than a third of them breeding there. Other reedbed specialities are the water rail, the reed warbler, and the very rare bearded tit, or bearded reedling, as it is sometimes known. One pair of bearded tits left over from a small overwintering flock lingered on to breed at Leighton Moss for the first time in 1973. Five years later the numbers had increased to 30 pairs. It is the distinctive black moustaches of the male tit hanging down on each side of the head which give rise to its common name. Within the reedbeds bearded tits feed on insects during the summer, changing their diet to the seeds of the reeds themselves in winter. These birds are also severely hit by hard weather, especially when heavy snowfalls or thick ice completely carpet the base of the reed beds – where the seeds collect.

Water rails are timid waders with long red bills, and are rarely seen except when a severe winter lures them out of the reedbeds to feed along the reed margins or even along the paths. When they take to the air their long legs dangle down below the body. The nest, built of dead reeds and sedges, is not unlike that of the moorhen, except it is much better hidden.

Mallard, shoveler, tufted duck, pochard and teal all breed at Leighton Moss but mallard far outnumber the other ducks. After the mallard have bred, they are joined by large numbers of other birds which move in from neighbouring breeding sites, since Leighton Moss is the main area where Morecambe Bay ducks congregate to moult. By midsummer, the mallard numbers swell to almost 2,000 birds. Teal have been encouraged to breed by the provision of larger areas of shallow water. Since duck shooting ceased in the reserve in 1979, there has been a marked increase in the numbers of over-wintering duck.

Both kingfishers and herons frequent the meres, and a heron can often be seen emerging from a reedbed to feed on fish – especially eels – in the open water. By inching its way through the mere, the heron can stalk an unsuspecting fish until it is within striking distance.

A colony of over 500 pairs of black-headed gulls now breed at Leighton Moss – chiefly on artificial islands created in two of the meres. Occasionally, a pair of these gulls decides to nest precariously on the ends of poles projecting above the water. In fact, the name of these gulls is appropriate only in summer, since in the winter plumage nearly all traces of the chocolate-brown head is lost.

Although Leighton Moss is quite rightly most widely proclaimed for the breeding successes of some very rare birds, there are many other less publicised attractions. Throughout the spring and summer months wild flowers bloom in an unbroken sequence, with dense stands of yellow flags flowering in May and June, followed by ragged robin, meadowsweet, and purple loosestrife. In shallow parts of the meres, quite extensive patches of marestail grow – providing the reeds are kept in check, while clumps of bulrushes stand upright like sentries and amphibious bistort spreads its floating leaves out over the surface.

Late in the evenings – especially in summer – flocks of starlings which congregate in nearby fields, swoop down over the reserve, and finally come to roost in the reedbeds in their thousands. The starlings are there every year, but Leighton Moss is a magnet for much less common species. The reserve never fails to provide a spectacle and there is always a possibility that a visit may coincide with a fleeting touch-down by a rare migrant such as an osprey or a marsh harrier.

Despite their name, black-headed gulls sport their dark heads only during the breeding season.

A COASTAL HILLTOP

From whichever angle you approach the peninsula on which it stands, Arnside Knott dominates the view. Jutting out into the sands of the Kent estuary astride the Cumbria-Lancashire border, this low limestone hill looks down onto the northern end of Morecambe Bay. It also faces some of the most spectacular mountains in England, which lie just a few miles to the north. Originating from a Saxon word, 'knott' means a rounded hill or rocky summit and is not infrequently incorporated into place names in the northwest of England. It is highly likely that the Iron Age hill folk, known as the Brigantes, occupied Arnside Knott at the time the Romans made their way northwards. From this vantage point they would have had excellent views of armies crossing the surrounding marshlands and tidal flats. On a clear day, especially in winter, when the deciduous trees are leafless, there are quite breathtaking views of the bay, with a splendid panorama of the Lake District peaks – snow-capped during cold winter spells – to the north, and the Ingleborough and Pen-y-ghent peaks to the northeast.

The area around Arnside and nearby Silverdale has been designated one of Outstanding Natural Beauty, and it attracts many visitors who come to enjoy the numerous self-guided walks which criss-cross the peninsula. Here and there traces of past small industries can be seen. Red patches of iron oxide in the soil are a legacy of the iron smelting. Some of the iron was locally mined, but most of the ore was imported from Scotland. After local timber supplies ran out, peat from Arnside and Silverdale Mosses, as well as Leighton Moss (see page 87) was used instead. Several limekilns remain today as proof of past lime-burning activities. Lime was made by packing alternate layers of limestone and poor quality coal – known as culm – on top of brushwood, inside the limekiln. Once the brushwood had been ignited, voluminous grey fumes billowed forth from the kiln. Farmers used the lime to help reduce the acidity of their cornfields.

While everyone who makes the effort to climb up one of the steep paths leading to the 159-metre (520-foot) high summit will be amply rewarded by the spectacular view, the Knott itself is of special interest to the geologist and the naturalist. The hill's limestone abounds with fossils, and the combination of grassland, scree, scrub and woodland, makes it an extremely rich area for plants. An energetic person might be able to sprint up to the top from the car park in half an hour, but they would miss a great deal on the way. The first time I climbed the Knott, I stopped to look and photograph so many times that it took me four hours to reach the summit!

Arnside Knott is made of carboniferous limestone, and in several places where the greyish-white rock is exposed to the elements it has been weathered by rain water and frost action (see page 20). This limestone originates from the accumulated limy skeletons of marine organisms which thrived in shallow seas during the Lower Carboniferous Period some 345 million years ago. The fossil remains of corals in

The magnificent view from Arnside Knott of the Kent estuary and the Lake District peaks beyond.

the fragmented limestone outcrops show that the seas were considerably warmer than they are today. The cockle-like shells of fossil marine brachiopods also occur in the Arnside limestone outcrop.

On the south-facing slopes of the Knott the limestone has broken up into scree slopes which overlie rocks worn smooth by moving ice. The scree, which is known locally as *shilloe*, must therefore have been formed after the glaciers had melted, probably by alternating freezing and thawing periods which fragments the rock. Like most screes, these slopes are difficult and dangerous to walk over, as the chunks of rock are easily sent rolling down the hillside.

Diminutive wild strawberries thrive on Arnside's stony scree slopes.

As might be expected, many of the wild flowers on Arnside are limestone-loving species such as wild orchids, rock rose, wild thyme, centaury, milkwort, ploughman's spikenard and felwort. But it may come as something of a surprise to find both ling and bell heather growing there too. These acid-loving plants grow in pockets which have become acid and peaty after the lime content has been washed out of the soil.

Throughout the summer, the succession of flowers on Arnside's sunny slopes attract many butterflies for which the area is especially noted. One day in June I spotted several brimstones on the wing and I also noticed plenty of alder buckthorns on which the brimstone caterpillars feed. When the first leaves of alder buckthorn burst open in spring, you may

be lucky enough to observe a female brimstone laying her yellow eggs – one at a time – beneath a leaf. Like the small tortoiseshells, the brimstone butterfly hibernates through the winter, and emerges only on the warmest days in early spring. Over twenty species of butterfly can be seen on the Knott including the orange-tip, green-veined white, the green hairstreak, both pearl-bordered fritillaries, the small copper, the common blue, the brown argus, the grayling and the large skipper. Arnside Knott is the most southerly site of only two in northern England for the Scotch argus butterfly, which is not uncommon in Scotland. The yellow-brown caterpillar has a dark brown central line and it feeds on grasses. The adults fly only when the sun is shining.

Another local insect speciality is the glowworm which is, in fact, a beetle. The wingless female looks so unlike a beetle that her true pedigree is easily mistaken. On a warm summer's night, the grass sparkles with the pale greenish light of the flightless females as they glow to attract their winged mates. Glow-worm lights are another sign that this is a limestone area, since these insects live mainly on slugs and snails which abound in places where calcium is present in the soil.

This abundant insect life, and the plentiful supply of cover, attracts many nesting birds. In the scrubby areas robins, wrens, blackbirds, thrushes, tits, bullfinches, willow warblers, blackcaps and yellowhammers all nest on Arnside; while nesting in the woodland are great spotted and green woodpeckers, tawny owls, wood pigeons, woodcock, jays, magpies and chiffchaffs.

Mammals are generally more secretive than birds and since most are active at dusk or at night, you are unlikely to come across many by day. If you are up early, however, you may be lucky enough to glimpse a roe deer, before it senses your presence and is away. In the autumn, red squirrels may be so intent on feeding on hazel nuts that you can watch them for quite a long time. Arnside is one of the few places where Britain's native red squirrel still outnumbers the much more widespread imported grey squirrel.

The Knott was once thickly wooded, for in 1820 extensive stands of larch were planted when the area was enclosed, but most of the larches were felled for pit props in the early part of this century. All that remains today are scattered stumps and a few trees, including the curious knotted trees near the summit. Standing side by side, two pairs of dead larches are now stark skeletons, but the horizontal connection between each pair of trunks is still clearly visible. The story goes that the freaks were formed more than a hundred years ago when two young lads from Silverdale tied each pair of saplings in a knot some 2 metres (6 feet) up from the ground. Over the years, the two trunks became united and fused by a common transverse trunk.

One naturally occurring evergreen shrub which is locally common at Arnside is juniper, which is by no means widespread throughout Britain. Another lime-lover, it grows on some of the chalk downlands in southern England as well as on Scottish moors. Nestling in among the needle-like leaves are small fruits which are green at first, turning blue-black when ripe. They were once used to counteract a viper's bite, but they are perhaps best known for providing flavour to gin.

Another evergreen which grows on the hill is the much larger yew tree. On some of the exposed slopes, the yews have been wind-pruned into bizarre lop-sided shapes which hug the hillside.

At one time, Arnside Knott was surrounded on three sides by relatively deep water, and during the reign of Henry VIII the town of Arnside was a bustling port, with intense

As a green-veined white butterfly momentarily alights on crosswort, it is backlit by the late afternoon sun.

shipping activity (by no means all legal) which took advantage of the eight inns sited along the Kent estuary. Today, two inns remain and the estuary has silted up so much that it is a rare sight to see a boat penetrating up beyond the railway viaduct. This was built in 1857 to carry the Furness railway across the mouth of the Kent estuary. Now, the viaduct is the chief obstacle to the tidal bore which sweeps up the estuary to Arnside during the high spring tides. Before the tidal wave reaches our shores, it travels across the Atlantic Ocean and is chan-

After this pair of pearl-bordered fritillaries have mated, the female will lay her eggs on wild violets.

nelled into the Irish Sea before it enters Morecambe Bay. Here, the land funnels the water so that it piles up into a huge wave which can be heard as a roar before the white crest is seen racing northwards up the bay. When the bore reaches the viaduct, it crashes against the supports sending a plume of sea water spray up and over any train which happens to be crossing at the time – no doubt quite startling for the rail passengers who are not expecting it! Other estuaries which experience tidal bores are the Ouse and Trent (Yorkshire), the Parrett (Somerset), the Solway Firth (this bore was described by Sir Walter Scott in *Redgauntlet*) and perhaps the most famous of all, the Severn bore. The best days for seeing a bore can be found by consulting local tide tables and seeing on what dates the biggest-ranging spring tides occur.

A view from Arnside Knott at low tide of the channels winding through the treacherous mud banks at the north end of Morecambe Bay.

Low-lying Arnside Moss used to be swamped by these high tides, so in 1776 an earth embankment was built to allow the land to be drained and reclaimed for agriculture.

The Kent is one of the swiftest rivers in England, in one stretch dropping more than 300 metres over 40 kilometres (985 feet over 25 miles). Once the river reaches the estuary, its course can be traced as it weaves its way through the exposed sand banks. These banks are the feeding grounds of the wading birds for which the estuary is famous. After several hours' exposure at low tide the sand dries and hardens making it quite unsuitable for waders. In winter many can be seen feeding immediately after the muds are exposed to the air, and in summer families of shelduck frequent the estuary, and if you are lucky, you may even spot a heron taking flounders or eels in the shallow water. Greylag geese, having bred in Iceland, move south to overwinter in the Kent estuary, feeding in the adjacent fields, and their characteristic V formation flight may sometimes be seen from lofty Arnside Knott.

For centuries before the viaduct was built, people crossed the Kent from Lancaster to Ulverston by fording the sands. Not infrequently, treacherous quicksands claimed the lives of coach horses and their passengers. As is the way of estuaries, the channels and banks constantly change, so that 'safe' channels suddenly become treacherous. Also, once the tide flows in over the flats it races faster than any person can run. Yet, the fishermen of Morecambe Bay earn their livelihood by knowing how to reach safely the best cockle beds and shrimping grounds. Cockles are still gathered in much the same way as a century or more ago except that the cart used to take the cocklers to the grounds is pulled by a tractor instead of a horse. The cockles are brought up to the surface of the wet sand by rocking a two handled plank to and fro, and the shellfish are then flicked into wicker baskets using a cramb, which is a curved three-pronged fork. In the past, all the time the cockles were being gathered, the horse had to be tethered just in case it wandered off and left the cocklers stranded.

March sees the start of the shrimping season which lasts through to May, followed by a second spell from August to November, when the shrimping is often done at night. Cedric Robinson, who has followed in his father's and grandfather's footsteps by fishing the bay, vividly describes a night when they went out shrimping. As the horses splashed their way through the water, they set off a spectacular phosphorescent glow (known locally as foxfire) which resembled a firework display. The foxfire light – caused by microscopic marine organisms – was good enough to see the shrimping nets and the shrimps in the boxes. In 1963, Mr Robinson was appointed as Queen's Guide to the Sands of Morecambe Bay which makes him reponsible for guiding up to 150 people at a time along the 13–19 kilometre (8–12 mile) walk across the bay. Overnight, the vagaries of the tides can change the pattern of the channels, so he must constantly reappraise and modify the best route across.

Whichever way you look at Arnside Knott, from the peak down to the estuary, or from the sands up to the hillside, the contrasts in terrain could not be greater, yet the hill is very much influenced by the sudden changes of the estuarine climate. The same is true for the wildlife of these two very different habitats, which lie so close together. In the summer months, flowers and butterflies thrive on the warm slopes of the Knott, while waders which spend their summers in arctic Europe wander over the estuary in search of food. Winters in Morecambe Bay are typically mild and it is then that the largest concentration of birds anywhere in Europe occurs. Over a quarter of a million waders take advantage of the 310 square kilometres (120 square miles) of mud and sand – the largest continuous intertidal area in Britain – exposed during low water. The spectacular lift-off of thousands of tiny birds wheeling back and forth across the mud flats has to be seen to be believed.

LIFE AMONG THE GRAVES

The parish church of Seamer, near Scarborough, was mentioned in the Domesday Book, evidence that there has been a church on the site for over 900 years. The original wooden church has long since disappeared, and only remnants remain of the Norman stone building. At one time, a spire was added, but this had to be pulled down after it was struck by lightning. Within the confines of their thick stone walls, churches such as St Martin's in Seamer offered a safe refuge for man in troubled times. Today, hundreds of years later, it is the turn of wildlife to use the church and its grounds as a refuge.

Thousands of holidaymakers annually pass through Seamer on their way to the Scarborough beaches, but few would ever guess its age, or that it was once a sizeable town. Although prehistoric remains show that man first inhabited the area 10,000 years ago, it was not until the Saxon period that Seamer village grew up. Later, in 1382, Richard II granted Henry Percy, the Lord of the Manor, and his heirs the right to hold a weekly market at Seamer Manor and a six-day annual fair on the feast of St Martin. It seems hard to believe today that for six days in July when Seamer Fair was in full swing, all the shops in Scarborough closed. The Fair was finally suppressed in 1627 after a lengthy legal battle with the Bailiffs and Burgesses of Scarborough who argued that it adversely affected the trading in their town. So Seamer town gradually shrank in importance, but the church remained.

Old churchyards up and down the country provide little oases where wild flowers and shrubs, as well as insects and birds, can flourish in today's swiftly changing countryside, where ancient hedgerows and old permanent pastures are few and far between. Whatever time you visit a churchyard there will be flowers worth seeing, but spring is undoubtedly best, when the ground may be covered by carpets of snowdrops, wild daffodils, primroses, bluebells or cowslips, and in damp areas, even fritillaries. I was first attracted to St Martin's churchyard early on a May morning when the ox-eye daisies – still in bud and pushing up from the outer wall – made me curious to find what lay beyond. As I climbed the steps up to the iron gate I could see an enticing show of spring meadow flowers in an old part of the churchyard. Here, where the grass is cut only a few times a year, plants such as cow parsley, dandelions, germander speedwell, crosswort and buttercups flourish in complete contrast to the grazed meadow outside the church boundary which is kept closely cropped by cattle.

In the churchyard itself a family of rabbits living beneath a table-top tomb had cropped down all the plants around their burrows, apart from the ground ivy. On warm evenings and early in the morning rabbits can be seen feeding and playing in the open, although they will not be active on windy or wet days. The Normans introduced rabbits into Britain from Europe, either keeping them enclosed in warrens on the mainland, or releasing them onto offshore islands such as Lundy in the Bristol Channel and Skomer off Dyfed. Inevitably, rabbits

The trees and grassy swards in St Martin's parish churchyard at Seamer harbour a profusion of wildlife.

Cowslips are one of many attractive wild flowers which have found a safe refuge in old churchyards.

escaped from the mainland warrens into the surrounding countryside, but initially their numbers grew only slowly. After the Enclosures Acts had been passed, hedgerows sprang up everywhere, providing ideal shelter for the wild rabbits. They became increasingly widespread

and eventually very abundant. Then in October 1953 a devastating disease reached Britain. Myxomatosis, carried via the rabbit flea, spread rapidly in the following two years wiping out as much as 99 per cent of the rabbit population in most areas. Once the rabbits disappeared, the scrub was no longer kept in check, so it began to spread, choking out wild orchids and other attractive flowers. After this epidemic, the rabbits began to win back as the virus weakened and some rabbits became resistant to the disease. It continues to break out annually, and grassland nature reserves, where there are small numbers of rabbits, have to be maintained by introducing grazing stock for limited periods. Some conservation bodies now use flocks of sheep for the job previously done for free by wild rabbits.

But repeated grazing – or mowing – limits the diversity of meadow plants, especially tall-stemmed species which never get a chance to flower, let alone set seed. Where parts of the churchyard, such as those adjacent to paths, or around recent graves, are repeatedly mown, short lawn-like grassy swards develop dotted with plants like daisies, plantains and hawk-weeds, all with flattened leafy rosettes which are untouched by the mower. If mowing is delayed until after the spring, perennial plants, such as the spring bulbs and cow parsley, are able to build up their underground food reserves which produce next year's flowers. In some churchyards the old practice of managing the grass by cutting with a scythe is still carried out, although it is now a rare sight to see sheep put out to graze in churchyards.

If churchyards are left completely untended, they soon become a complete wilderness as shrubs invade and grass and ivy scramble over old headstones. The best situation for wildlife is where there is a balance between the neatly tended recent graves and the untouched older corners. Then, within the confines of churchyard walls, a host of animals can seek refuge. During damp weather, slugs and snails will emerge by day and can often be seen crawling over gravestones, but during dry spells they retreat into damper areas such as the grasses around the base of the stones. Small mammals such as mice and voles live in underground burrows, emerging to forage on a variety of shoots and fruits. Bank voles are amazingly agile and will climb up branches several metres off the ground in order to reach a clump of hips or haws. These mammals in turn provide food for predatory birds such as kestrels, the tawny and barn owls, which sometimes use church towers for nesting, providing the belfries are not fenced with wire netting. Belfries, as well as the church itself, are also used by bats for roosting. Even wolves have played their part in the natural history of the graveyard. Extinct in Britain for centuries, they once roamed our mainland, and in Highland graveyards they dug up corpses during severe winter weather. Small wonder that several of the Summer Isles off Scotland's northwest coast were used as burial grounds.

Apart from where graves have been dug, churchyard grassland has remained intact since the ground was consecrated – often centuries ago. Unlike modern meadows which are all too often ploughed and fertilized every few years to provide a more productive crop for stock, natural grassland sports a succession of wild flowers right through summer, starting with the short-stemmed daisies and ending with the long-stemmed umbellifers, such as cow parsley and hogweed.

For some of our rarer wild flowers, notably wild orchids of chalk grassland, churchyards may be the only suitable site within a locality surrounded by arable land. These and other lime-loving plants such as quaking grass, and burnet saxifrage, may also be more abundant within a churchyard than outside it because the calcium content of the soil is increased by the

On an overcast day a snail emerges from its moist hideout and crawls across a gravestone.

weathering of limestone graves as well as from buried bones.

By no means all churchyard flowers are wild however, and more often than not, garden flowers which have been planted on graves will invade the churchyard, providing additional

At night the haunting hoot of the tawny owl can be heard from country churchyards to city parks as it calls out to defend its territory.

colour. For example, bright pink everlasting pea now romps over the wilder part of Brompton Cemetery in London, and many churchyards have a clump of rosemary (for remembrance). The wider the range of flowers in a churchyard, the more species of insects such as butterflies and beetles will be attracted to it.

As well as flowers, churchyards harbour shrubs and trees, which provide shade, a source of food and nesting sites for birds. It is no accident that yew trees often feature in churchyards; this evergreen tree was once regarded as a symbol of everlasting life, and yew sprigs used to be buried with the dead. Even in the pre-Christian era, the yew was regarded as sacred. It seems likely that some of the earliest Christian churches were built on sites of pagan worship, so that some ancient churchyard yews are estimated to be more than 2,000 years old. No other British tree grows to such an age. The biggest specimens occur in parish churchyards in a distinct zone stretching from northwest Wales down to southeast England. They can also be seen outside churchyards, but rarely do they thrive as a pure woodland, although Kingley Vale National Nature Reserve on the Sussex South Downs contains a magnificent yew wood with a grove of 800 to 1,000-year-old trees. Being evergreen, yews cast a heavy shadow all year round, so that little grows beneath them at Kingley Vale.

Yew wood is elastic but strong, a combination of properties which made it ideal for long bows. But since English yews produce timber with more knots in it than European-grown trees, this was probably less suitable as long bow wood. Nearly every part of the tree – the leaves, bark and seeds – contain a poison called taxine, which can be fatal to livestock, but trees

planted within the confines of the churchyard walls would be unlikely to be reached by cattle. Yews sited adjacent to the church path leading up to the porch were no doubt planted to provide shelter for the pall-bearers.

Instead of producing male and female flowers on the same tree, yew trees are either male or female, and when the yellow male flowers open early in spring, clouds of yellow pollen grains can be seen wafting away from the sombre green branches. Pollen therefore reaches the female flowers purely by chance, but so much is produced, that it allows for a high percentage falling elsewhere. Once the flowers have been pollinated, the seeds begin to develop and finally the fleshy outer cup – the aril – turns a bright red colour. This non-poisonous part of the yew is highly attractive to birds, especially mistle thrushes and blackbirds, and they gorge themselves in autumn on yews, passing out the poisonous seeds in their droppings, to disperse the seeds away from the parent tree.

Old tombstones are well worth a closer look for their own special plant life. As stones are weathered, especially around their inscriptions, they provide minute resting places for lichen spore packages. Lichens are really dual plants, an alga and a fungus living so intimately that their cells are completely intermingled. Growth is slow; often only 1 millimetre (0.04 inch) being added to the radius of a circular encrusting lichen in a year, but lichens often live through several centuries. Limestone and sandstone tombstones both have natural roughened surfaces on which spores and seeds are more likely to get lodged, whereas the smooth surfaces of polished marble and granite harbour few if any growths.

Encrusting orange lichens are one of many attractive tombstone lichens which will flourish only in pollution-free air in sunny situations. Having no roots, they must absorb all their nutrients from the air, which makes them

As the days lengthen in late spring, parts of the churchyard at Seamer are swathed in the umbrella-shaped flower-heads of cow parsley.

excellent indicators of atmospheric pollution. In churchyards adjacent to industrial cities, or even many miles away but in direct line of the prevailing winds, lichens are few in number and small in size.

Lichens generally prefer growing in well lit situations, as on the upper sunny portions of headstones, because only a small part of the plant – the algal partner – contains the green pigment chlorophyll and is able to manufacture carbohydrate foods in the presence of sunlight. In return, the fungal partner provides shelter and moisture for the alga.

It was an early Christian custom to bury the dead with their feet towards the west to face the Risen Christ on the Resurrection Morning; therefore, providing old headstones have not been moved from their original positions, their broad sides will be orientated east-to-west. Also, old graves will be found on the south side of the church, since the cold, north side was regarded as belonging to the Devil. But lack of space in old churchyards may mean that old headstones have to be moved elsewhere. Inside the walls of Seamer churchyard, old headstones have been stacked so closely that little sunlight now reaches their broad sides, and hence few, if any, lichens are able to flourish in this shady situation.

Mosses prefer growing in damper and more shady locations, either at the bases of head-stones or in deep cracks where the rain is continually channelled. Leaky gutters or drain-pipes also encourage mosses, which can appear on shady church roofs as well as walls. A cobbled churchyard path is somehow not quite complete unless each cobble is surrounded by a green mossy border. Cracks and crevices which develop in walls, when old mortar begins to

Over the decades encrusting lichens have colonised the surfaces of these old headstones.

crumble away between stones, are places where mosses are most likely to take hold. Wall crevices also provide permanent shelter for a host of small invertebrate animals and short-term nesting sites for birds as well as several small mammals.

Although the management of churchyards will vary up and down the country, depending not least on the finances available in the parish, it is a remarkable fact that some 10,000 sub-stantially medieval churches like St Martin's still remain in Britain. Each churchyard is an invaluable history book, allowing us glimpses into past local communities, and today many are undiscovered wildlife havens, islands of undisturbed ground in Britain's ever-changing landscape.

SURVIVAL
IN AN INDUSTRIAL SETTING

In theory, land adjacent to an industrial conurbation, which is bisected by a spaghetti-like maze of railway lines, would seem most unsuitable as a nature reserve. Yet Potteric Carr*, near Doncaster, is proof that industrialisation need not go hand in hand with the destruction of a wildlife haunt. This reserve, which is managed by the Yorkshire Naturalists' Trust, now contains a plethora of habitats – open water, reed fen, grassland, willow carr, living birch and oak woodland, dead flooded woodland, embankments and waste ground. All this has been created through a combination of man's past activities, and a great deal of more recent voluntary work, determination and careful planning. Together, these habitats harbour a diverse collection of animals and plants, although few people who hurtle across the reserve on one of the 76 high-speed trains which leave Doncaster daily would appreciate the richness of this chequered site.

Originally a swamp, Potteric Carr was later drained, but parts of it have now become submerged once again as a result of mining subsidence which began in the 1960s. This flooding has resulted in both gains and losses. Fenland plants which had survived only in the dykes during the earlier drier period, when the land was drained and farmed, could spread out once the new wetlands were formed. This movement has provided botanists with an

opportunity to study the rate at which such plants move into new habitats. I noticed celery-leaved crowfoot – a relative of the buttercup with tiny yellow petals – flourishing at Potteric Carr where the roots are permanently submerged in waterlogged ground or in the drains. On the other hand, bog myrtle, marsh andromeda and cranberry are plants which have completely disappeared from Potteric Carr, because their bogland habitat has been lost.

As at Fairburn Ings (page 73) permanent water has attracted wildfowl into the area, but it has also killed off quite a large area of oak and birch woodland. The dead trees, which include some of the oldest in the reserve, remain standing as a ghostly forest, the bare branches providing convenient roosting perches, while the cavities are used by hole-nesting birds. Tits, treecreepers, starlings and woodpeckers all nest here, but as each year passes the rate of decay increases as more and more fungi invade the old timber.

Potteric Carr lies 3 kilometres (2 miles) southeast of industrial Doncaster, but in the sixteenth century it lay within Hatfield Chase. This was the largest royal deer chase in the country, a part of Sherwood Forest with majestic oaks scattered over it and the surrounding hills. Lying only 8 metres (26 feet) above sea level, Potteric Carr was always marshy and in those days it was virtually an impenetrable

* Public access is limited. For further details contact the Yorkshire Naturalists' Trust, 20 Castlegate, York YO1 1RP.

The industrial backcloth of Doncaster rears up behind the nature reserve at Potteric Carr.

Persistent flooding has reduced what was once a living woodland of oak and birch to a mass of gaunt skeletons with relatively little value to wildlife.

boggy morass. This was precisely the type of habitat which was then known in Yorkshire and Lincolnshire as a 'carr'; today the word has been adopted by botanists to apply more specifically to alder or willow woodlands which develop on swampy ground all over Britain.

Several attempts were made to drain this swamp, notably in 1626 by the Dutchman Vermuyden, who is perhaps best known for his engineering work on the Bedford levels in East Anglia. Duck decoys originated in Holland where they were used for catching wild duck for food, and it is most likely that the idea of building a decoy pond on Potteric Carr marshes

in 1657 was initiated by the Dutchmen who came over with Vermuyden. Since south Doncaster marshes were then famous for their wildfowl, Potteric Carr was an obvious site for one. Duck decoys were designed so that birds were attracted into a central area of open water from which 'pipes' – curved tapering ditches covered by a netting tunnel – radiated out. Curious ducks were lured into the open end of a pipe by following the movement of a decoy dog, which appeared momentarily and then disappeared behind screens set at right angles along the length of the pipe. Once plenty of ducks were inside the pipe, the sudden appearance of the decoyman at the open end made the ducks move further down towards the narrow end of the pipe where they were caught in a net. The Potteric Carr decoy covered 2·5 hectares, or more precisely '6 acres, 3 rods and 23 perches', and had six pipe nets radiating out from the central decoy lake. The duck decoy was used for just over a century, chiefly during the winter months – from October to March – when large numbers of wildfowl homed in on the Carr. All the profits gained from selling the decoy ducks went to help the poor people of Doncaster.

By the mid 1700s the area was becoming more and more disturbed, on the one hand by commoners' cattle put out to graze and on the other by noblemen participating in stag and fox hunts across the Carr. Eventually, in the 1760s, most of the land was drained (not too effectively at first for some horses drowned in the

Clumps of bird's-foot trefoil enliven the railway rubble and provide food for blue butterflies.

boggy ground) but by the end of the century it had been converted from swamp to arable land and only a small portion – 2 hectares (5 acres) – of the original bog plants remained around the old decoy. As the land dried out, hedges and woodlands were planted, and a typical patchwork landscape developed.

But the changes to the area brought about in the succeeding century were drastic compared to those which had gone before. The year 1849, when the Great Northern Railway was built right across the Carr and through the centre of the decoy, saw the birth of Doncaster as a railway capital. Increasing numbers of trains encouraged the growth of the local coal industry and sidings for the coal trains were later built on the site of the decoy. The railway embankments, which were constructed of magnesian lime-

stone in the final bout of railway building between 1880 and 1908, have provided a suitable terrain for cowslips, yellow-wort, pyramidal orchids and ploughman's spikenard – all chalk-loving plants.

As more and more link and loop lines were built, the area became a maze of track. But when the volume of railway freight traffic declined after the war, some of these lines were closed, completely isolating portions of land which were no longer economical to farm.

The dramatic return of wildfowl to Potteric Carr in the 1960s, after extensive areas of open water appeared when the ground subsided, greatly enriched the area, prompting the Yorkshire Naturalists' Trust to take over the tenancy of part of it. But within three years, it became known that the proposed route of the M18 Motorway would cut right through the centre of the reserve. Fortunately, the motorway was finally re-routed, but only after a tremendous lobby by conservationists. When in 1975–6, British Railways constructed a new railway through the reserve, they co-operated with the Trust so that the work created the least possible disturbance. But, still in the seventies, a third blow was to hit Potteric: it was selected as an ideal place to store surplus rainwater run-off, and the construction of the deep drains and the pumping station created a good deal of disturbance. However, if all goes according to plan, future water levels will be carefully controlled for the benefit of the wildlife.

I knew as soon as I arrived at Potteric on May 20th 1982 that a rare bird had touched down, for the car park was alive with 'twitchers' brandishing powerful binoculars and telescopes. These birdwatchers are prepared to travel from one part of the country to another as soon as they hear through the grapevine that a rare bird has been sighted. Once seen, it can then be ticked off on the all-important species total. On this occasion it was a red-footed falcon, a rare

Wading out to feed, by probing its long bill in the mud, a snipe is mirrored in the shallow water.

visitor from Eastern Europe and Russia, which was causing all the excitement.

I scurried past the crowd in search of Potteric Carr's more regular inhabitants, and I soon spotted one recently-emerged cinnabar moth after another resting on plants on either side of the path. Moving on to the rubble ground adjacent to the railway lines two plants were in full flower. The track was decorated with the prostrate yellow blooms of bird's-foot trefoil or eggs-and-bacon and the upright white spikes of horseradish. Bird's-foot trefoil is the food plant of the caterpillars of the common blue butterfly, and so it was no surprise to learn that this species does occur here. Considering the price of horseradish sauce, many more people might be tempted to seek out this widespread plant growing for free on waste ground – outside reserve areas – if they could recognise it. Long before the flowering spikes appear, large dark green crinkly-edged leaves spring up on road-side verges, railway embankments and derelict building sites. It is the deep tap root which is the basic ingredient for the sauce; but if you do succeed in digging it up, you will find that the fumes it emits when peeled make those of raw onions pale into insignificance!

Frogs, toads and newts all breed in the pools and dykes and here grass snakes and water voles can also be seen swimming. After smooth newts have finished breeding, they crawl out of the water and can often be found beneath debris on embankments.

An exciting discovery in 1974 was that Britain's smallest mammal, the harvest mouse – once thought to be rare in Yorkshire – was quite common on one part of the reserve. This agile little mouse uses its prehensile tail to climb up and grasp on to the tallest of reeds. It builds its nests in grasses, reeds or cereal crops, by weaving shredded leaves with parallel leaf veins across a cluster of stiff-stemmed grasses. The inside of the nest may be lined with feathers or thistle seeds. From three to eight blind and naked young are born, each one weighing under 1 gramme (0·035 ounce). Harvest mice are most active at dusk and dawn, although in winter, when they are very susceptible to losing heat from their bodies, they are more active during the day. Each mouse needs to eat the equivalent of 30 per cent of its own weight per day simply to keep its body at the right temperature. Very little is known about the type of food which wild harvest mice eat, but captive animals will feed on seeds, fruit and insects. One unusual natural food source is the nectar from cowslips which the harvest mouse obtains by climbing up the flower stem and eating through the base of each bloom.

The harvest mouse is difficult to see, but Potteric Carr's main attractions, waterfowl and waders, can be observed quite easily from strategically placed hides. Several different kinds of duck can be seen throughout the year: mallard, teal, garganey, shoveler and tufted duck all breed here, while gadwall, wigeon, pintail and goldeneye are occasional visitors. Soft mud attracts feeding waders, particularly snipe in winter, and with the arrival of early summer, sand martins take advantage of it for building their nests.

Ironically, it is as a direct result of mining – one of the many ways in which man has exploited the area – that wildfowl have, once again, returned to Potteric Carr, although the present-day wetlands represent only a small fraction of the original swamp. This site is one which could so easily have died several times over, but after surviving the Industrial Revolution and the coming of both railways and motorways, it remains today as a prime example of what can be achieved by means of compromises on both sides. It is to be hoped that the wildlife of this reserve on a city's edge can now look forward to a more secure and tranquil future.

OUR HEDGEROW HERITAGE

For many people, the hedgerow is the hallmark of the British countryside. As you move through lowland Britain, not only does the landscape change, but also the type of hedgerow with it. There are pure beech hedges on raised banks in Exmoor National Park, ash trees and Midland hawthorn in the Midlands, pollarded willows beside the Sedgemoor dykes in Somerset, and sombre pine shelter-belts in the agricultural Norfolk Brecklands.

The undulating Yorkshire Wolds are a patchwork of fields, bordered in the main by low neatly-clipped hawthorn hedges. In this part of the country old overgrown hedges with a wide assortment of wild flowers, shrubs and trees are comparatively rare, but several do still exist. Along one stretch in the parish of Walkington, typical woodland plants such as dog's mercury, bluebell, wild garlic, wood anemone and wild arum confirm that the strip of road-side scrub is a relic of an old woodland, since these plants move into new hedgerows very slowly, if at all.

This hedgerow scrub, which once served as a parish boundary, is all that is left of the old woodland which was cleared to provide agricultural land. The 1795 enclosure map of Walkington parish marks a woodland adjacent to the hedgerow but records show that most of this was felled between 1795 and 1855. The small area of woodland which does exist there today cannot be original since young ash and sycamore predominate and there are no old trees at all.

Hedges existed as far back as Anglo-Saxon times, and in the Middle Ages they were plentiful enough to be used as a source of fuel, but most of our existing hedges originate from the time of the Enclosure Acts. These Acts spanned three centuries and a total of 5,000 were passed, the majority between 1760 and 1820. They not only transformed the British landscape, but also resulted in commoners losing their small strips of land in large open fields. They were compensated with an equivalent amount of land or holding which had to be enclosed by hedges within a year of it being awarded to them. As the land became enclosed into small fields, so the hedgerow pattern developed.

Today, a hedge is thought of as a line of closely planted living shrubs or low trees forming a boundary between pieces of land or between fields and roads. Ancient hedges, on the other hand, were dead ones made from cut thorns or brushwood which eventually rotted away and had to be replaced, unlike the permanent planted hedges which superseded them. The heyday of the enclosures provided a boom for nurseries supplying hedging seedlings – notably hawthorn, which was, and still is, the most widely planted hedgerow shrub. It is a plant which provides food for a plethora of animals: the leaves alone are eaten by nearly 100 species of moth larvae as well as the hawthorn sawfly; the attractive white flowers (known as may) are visited by a host of insects – bees, flies and butterflies – and the red berries are eaten by the hawthorn shieldbug and by small mammals and birds. May Day is still

When hedgerow fruits ripen in autumn they make a rich harvest for birds and mammals.

celebrated in some parts of the country on May 1st by traditional ceremonies incorporating garlands of the white may flowers. Even the thorns of hawthorns have their uses. For centuries man has used them as tools for jobs such as boring holes, catching fish, tatooing the skin and extracting winkles from their shells. Thorny

Beside a country road, blackthorn flowers profusely in an old untrimmed hedge in April before the other shrubs have leafed out.

leafless branches were used in the kitchen for impaling mushroom caps so they could slowly dry out in the warm air.

Hawthorn may be planted up as a single species hedge, or it may be mixed with blackthorn or holly. All these plants bear either thorny stems or prickly leaves and so help to make the hedge stockproof. Trees were also planted in hedges, either as a source of timber, or for poles by being pollarded, which entails periodically lopping the tree some 2·5–3·5

The hawthorn shieldbug lives up to its name by feeding on hawthorn fruits and leaves which it pierces with its sharp beak.

metres (8–12 feet) above ground level to promote the growth of multiple stems.

English elms were a feature of many hedgerows in south and east England – notably East Anglia where Constable often incorporated them into his landscapes. They are easily propagated from cuttings, and once established, spread rapidly by means of suckers. Elms are quite majestic trees, but now that Dutch elm disease – caused by a fungus which is transmitted from one tree to another by the elm bark beetle – has devastated so many of our elms, their gaunt dead skeletons are becoming a familiar sight. Whatever trees replace them in hedgerows, it is doubtful if they will ever match the elm's magnificent shape and autumnal colouration. Before Dutch elm disease struck our elms, nearly half of England's hardwood timber could be found growing in hedges.

Regardless of whether a planted hedge started life as a single species or as a mixture of species, other shrubs, as well as wild flowers, will gradually move in. Just how quickly will depend on the type of the soil, and on whether the adjacent land is woodland or farmland. Woodland shrubs such as hazel and field maple often appear in hedges, their fruits dispersed by animals and wind respectively. Over 500 plants have been recorded in British hedgerows, about half of which grow regularly in this habitat. On lime-rich ground, guelder rose, dogwood, wild clematis and buckthorn are typical hedgerow

On an unkempt verge which has escaped the mower,
bluebells, yellow archangel and stitchwort combine to
form this eye-catching display.

plants. Blackthorn, wild roses, bramble, wild
pear, wild cherry, crab apple and rowan, like
hawthorn, all belong to the rose family, and can
be found in hedges throughout Britain.

The word 'hedge' has been incorporated into
the names of many animals and plants, among
them are the hedgehog, hedge sparrow and
hedge brown butterfly. Several delightful less
well known local names of hedgerow plants
incorporate the word, such as 'hedgehogs' from
Somerset for goosegrass, 'hedge feathers' from
Yorkshire for fruiting wild clematis and 'hedge
maids' from East Anglia for ground ivy, and
indeed the word 'hawthorn' is derived from
'hedgethorn'.

Dating old hedgerows can give a fascinating
glimpse of rural history. This can be done by
consulting old documents, notably enclosure or
tithe maps. If these are not available, a useful
(but approximate) way of dating a hedge is to
count the number of different kinds of woody
plants – not their seedlings – on one side only
of a 27–metre (30–yard) stretch. This figure is
then used in the following formula, devised by
Dr Max Hooper, for determining the age of a
hedge from its variety of woody species:

(Number of species × 110) + 30 years = Age of hedge

Even then, the result can only be regarded as an
estimate to the nearest 200 years. In general,
older hedges contain more woody species than
young hedges, but if either a variety of shrubs
were originally planted in a hedge, or it is a relic
of a former woodland, then erroneously high
figures will be obtained by using this method.

Whichever way you look at them, recent
hedgerow statistics make depressing reading.
Until the middle of this century, hedgerows
were abundant over lowland Britain covering

nearly 200,000 hectares (500,000 acres) or twice
the area of our official nature reserves. During
the period 1946–63, some 8,000 kilometres
(5,000 miles) of hedges were lost on average per
year, so that during the last 25 years roughly a
quarter of our hedges have been removed.
Modern farming methods have been chiefly
responsible for this dramatic loss. The development of large-scale combine harvesting makes
it more economical for an arable farmer to
operate with a smaller number of larger fields.
The machinery requires more room for man-
oeuvering and since the average width of a
hedge is 2 metres (6 feet), the removal of 5
kilometres (3 miles) of hedges provides an
additional hectare (2·5 acres) of arable land. As
labour costs increase, so does the cost of
maintaining a hedge and some farmers regard
hedges as a source of pests and weeds which
may invade their crops. But hedges undoubtedly bring benefits too. In windy areas they act as
shelter belts; the small daffodil fields in the
Isles of Scilly are protected by 7-metre (23-foot)
high hedges. They may also help to prevent soil
erosion. Dramatic proof of this can be seen in
the Fens, where shrinkage of the peaty soils
coupled with wind erosion has resulted in field
levels dropping several metres below that of the
metalled roads.

Until as recently as 1972, farmers could apply
for Ministry of Agriculture grants to cover part of
the cost of grubbing up their hedges, providing
this resulted in a more efficiently run farm.
However, by no means all hedgerows are
removed by farmers; some disappear as motorways are constructed or factories and housing
estates are built. Today, field boundaries in
Britain total almost 1·6 million kilometres (1
million miles), about 65 per cent of which are
hedges harbouring an estimated 10 million
breeding birds.

It is ironical that farmers are now able to get
financial assistance for planting new hedges

and also for renovating old ones. Even though new hedges are being planted, it takes a long time – a century or more – to produce a hedge with a reasonable diversity of plants and animals. There could not be a greater contrast between the relic woodland hedge at Walkington and a new hedge on the opposite side of the

A cock linnet, with his distinctive red breast, returns to his nest surrounded by a bower of brambles and honeysuckle.

road, which is pure cherry laurel. The shiny evergreen leaves, containing hydrocyanic acid, were used by entomologists in their insect-killing bottles, so this kind of hedge will support the minimum of wildlife. The old hedge, on the other hand, harbours copious wild plants and animals. The richness of the wildlife of this hedge is partly a result of its great age, and partly because it is not severely pruned back, but left to grow untended. When hedgerows are cut in autumn or winter, the youngest branches

The nocturnal dormouse is rarely seen in the hazel thickets in which it lives, except at twilight.

are removed, which will mean that some shrubs will not flower during the next summer.

Early in the year, hazel catkins in the old hedge blow in the breeze, shedding their pollen on to the tiny red female flowers which, by autumn, develop into cob nuts. As the spring flowers open beneath the shrubs, the hedge resounds with bird song. By summer, the most conspicuous sounds are made by insects: bees and hoverflies buzzing, and crickets and grass-hoppers stridulating. Autumn is the time when I most enjoy hedgerows, as the leaves and fruits take on dramatic hues. The Walkington hedge is a riot of colour in autumn – the brilliant scarlet

rosehips, wild arum and guelder rose, the wine-red haws, the scarlet-turning-to-black wayfaring tree fruit, the green, red and black blackberries, the green-turning-to-black elder berries, and the black berries and red leaves of dogwood. Small bank voles, as well as birds such as blackirds, thrushes, redwings and fieldfares, feast on ripe fruits. Even in winter, hedgerows are by no means lifeless; many birds will perch on the highest parts to gain a vantage point, while holes in larger trees provide roost-ing sites.

Old hedgerows need preserving more than ever now that so many have been lost this century. Felling is not the only threat that they face: herbicides applied to fields can blow on to hedgerows and kill the more delicate plants. If this happens, the bottom step in the hedgerow food pyramid shrinks and so less food is available for the plant-eating animals. We now know the far-reaching cumulative effects which pesticides have on birds of prey such as sparrowhawks and peregrines, but who knows what effects herbicides may have on hedge-rows? It is for this reason that the Conservation Committee of the Botanical Society of the British Isles is staging a Hedgerows and Herbi-cides Survey. Hedgerows are so diverse and widespread that this will be an enormous undertaking, but we still have a great deal to learn about the permanent residents and tem-porary visitors in these wildlife corridors that span the country.

A GROUSE MOOR

Ilkley Moor, made famous by the nineteenth century folksong 'On Ilkla Moor baht 'at' ('On Ilkley Moor without a hat') is without doubt one of the best known moors in England, but seen from the road, it is something of an anti-climax. The initial impression is one of a virtually feature-less, windswept expanse, dotted with a few rocky outcrops which, perhaps, inspired Brigantian tribesmen who settled in Ilkley during the Iron Age to give it the name Llecan, meaning 'stony place'. To appreciate the natural life on this open, virtually treeless moorland on the eastern flank of the Pennines, you must be prepared to leave the road and tramp among the heather and crowberry, perhaps following the very same paths trodden by Stone and Bronze Age man, who lived and earned their livelihood on the Moor in all weathers many centuries ago.

One April morning I was up before breakfast to photograph red grouse which live on the upper slopes. As I followed a track I passed last year's dead bracken fronds and a few bilberry plants which I identified with difficulty, for their bare leafless stems had been browsed so closely to the ground that they bore little resemblance to the erect 50-centimetre (20-inch) high plants which flourish ungrazed on my local Surrey heathlands.

In damp hollows I suddenly came across bright green patches of the bog moss *Sphagnum* which thrives in acidic pools of dark peaty water. The large hollow cells inside the leaves can soak up water 16–20 times their own dry weight, and the dry bog moss plants are such an effective sponge that they were used as absorbent dressings to mop up wounds. During the First World War Britain alone used a million *Sphagnum* dressings each month. Peat deposits which develop from the accumulation of bog mosses (and other plants) are used both as a source of fuel (an Irish power station is powered solely by peat) and by gardeners as a compost.

Cotton grass, with its conspicuous white fluffy seed heads, also indicates boggy ground underfoot. On other moors, these white bobbles have inspired local names such as white path moss and featherbed. Wherever they grow, they can be spotted from afar, and so it is much easier to circumnavigate boggy patches where cotton grass occurs.

Other less common plants of boggy areas include bog asphodel with its attractive yellow flower spikes, cranberry (which is unfortunately too rare to make it worthwhile to collect enough fruits to make a sauce), and the pale lilac-flowered marsh violet. However, one of the most bizarre bogland plants must be the insectivorous sundew, which traps insects on its sticky leaves as surely as fly paper. You will find no trace of sundew in the colder months for this annual plant dies down in the autumn. Come the late spring, the first of the red leaves emerge and unfurl their sticky tentacles ready for an unwary insect which chances to alight on the plant. Once trapped, its body is digested by chemicals released by the sundew, which then absorbs nitrogen-rich substances from the insect, lacking in the waterlogged boggy ground.

In April, Ilkley Moor is still covered by a brown carpet of dead bracken.

125

The straggling evergreen plant which I could not ignore on Ilkley however was crowberry, which was spreading everywhere it could send out shoots. Crowberry is a plant of mountains

Growing through a blanket of Sphagnum *moss, the sticky leaves of a sundew plant mean sure death for any unwary insect which settles on them.*

and moorlands in the north and west of Britain, extending as far south as Dartmoor. Crowberry plants are either male or female, and so, like holly, the round berry-like fruits are produced only on female plants after the flowers have been pollinated. The fruits are at first green, turning black when ripe. They are eaten by many moorland birds, notably by red grouse, which also feed on the young shoots. But it is young heather shoots to which grouse are particularly partial, while they nest among old heather plants, so that small portions of grouse-managed moors, such as Ilkley, are burnt annually to remove shrubby plants and to encourage the growth of new shoots. This burning must be carefully controlled so that the plants are not completely killed off. Known as 'muirburn' in Scotland, the practice is prohibited during spring and summer. The result of 10-year rotational burning of small patches is to produce a mosaic of different-aged heather, so that the game birds always have some young shoots for feeding and older plants for nesting as well as for cover and shelter. All this is in aid of the 'Glorious Twelfth', when the grouse shooting season commences. For the four months following August 12th, shooting parties, together with their beaters who put up the grouse towards the shooters, tramp over the moor in search of their quarry.

No other bird is so characteristic of the open, treeless moorland scene than the red grouse, which is also known as the 'moor bird'. Its own distribution, which is dependent on the suitability of the terrain and food supplies, in turn influences the distribution of one kind of beetle which lives solely in grouse droppings!

The grouse is a highly territorial bird. The male, or cock, stakes out his territory in the autumn by suddenly leaping into the air and skimming low over the moor with down-curved outstretched wings and tail. When challenging a rival cock, he uses a harsh barking call sounding something like 'go back, go back'. Once a territory has been won, the dark red-brown cock remains with his lighter-coloured hen until the following summer, after they have reared their young. During my early morning walk, I approached quite close to a pair of grouse by inching my way forwards on my stomach. The cock was remarkably unperturbed, slowly walking forward a few steps and then pausing to feed, whereas the hen froze in the bracken.

Although successful introductions of red grouse have been made on Exmoor and Dartmoor, the population in Britain as a whole has been decreasing since 1940. There are many reasons for the decline of the grouse, the main one being the deterioration in the heather quality with the decrease in the number of keepers working on the grouse moors.

Whether grouse are killed by a gun or not, they are short-lived birds, with some 65 per cent dying within the first year of life. In severe winters, when snow completely blankets the heather, grouse will move down to lower ground, to feed, returning to the higher ground as soon as the snow melts.

Ilkley Moor is a fine example of how an area of common moorland can be jointly used as a grouse moor and as a public leisure ground. Sharing the moor with the sheep and the grouse are not only walkers and naturalists, but also orienteers, rock climbers, hang-gliders and, not least, the hundreds of runners who swarm up the steep slopes each summer in the annual fell race.

Having reached the 402-metre (1,318-foot) high summit, on a fine day you can see York Minster 56 kilometres (35 miles) away to the northeast and also the top of Ingleborough to the northwest. But it is worth remembering that, as on any high ground, the weather on Ilkley Moor is unpredictable. It can be warm and sunny in Ilkley town while winds and even hail rage across the high tops.

Grouse feast on the ripe black fruits of crowberry as well as on its green shoots.

However, the climate on the moor has not always been as inhospitable as it is today. Since the pollen grains of each kind of plant have their own distinctive shape, they can be used to build up a picture of past plant communities. Examination of pollen grains preserved in peat

since prehistoric times shows that when Meso-
lithic man was roaming over the moor, in the
middle of the Stone Age between 12,000 and
3,000 BC, birch trees flourished on the upper
slopes, while lower down grew stands of oak
and alder in a much milder climate than today.
Apart from the odd holly, rowan or hawthorn,
the native trees have now gone and the most
obvious trees are the groups of pines which
have been planted beneath the Crags. Although
present in small numbers, nomadic Stone Age
man, with primitive tools such as scrapers and
arrowheads inevitably brought some changes to
the natural scene. Later on, during the Neolithic
period or New Stone Age (3,000–1,800 BC) man
was a farmer-hunter, and axe heads found lower
down the slopes indicate this is where he lived,
probably making forays to the higher ground to
graze his animals and for hunting.

From about 1,500 BC, Bronze Age man lived
on the moor. He left behind numerous examples of 'cup and ring' marks on stones
roughly following the 300 metre (1,000 foot)
contour line, which suggests they were made
along a well defined route. The markings were
laboriously pecked out of the gritstone rock by
chipping with a heavy stone tool and can be
distinguished from the deeper hollows with
steeper sides formed by the action of water.
Each cup is about 5 centimetres (2 inches) in
diameter and is encircled by one or more outer
rings, often linked to wavy lines. The significance of these primitive markings is not known
although similar ones have been found, made
by other civilizations in such far-flung places as
America, Madagascar and Fiji.

The Romans occupied Ilkley from 87–400 AD,
and after them came the Angles, Saxons, Danes
and Normans. The Romans built one of their
many auxiliary Pennine forts at Ilkley which they

*A red grouse cock is a highly territorial bird which spends
much time chasing off intruders.*

called Olicana. Both the fort and the camp were carefully sited so they were bordered by the River Wharfe to the north and by a stream on either side, although all that is left of the fort today is part of the west wall.

Before the Middle Ages the flooded valley of the River Wharfe was a forest-fringed swamp shrouded in mists but this swampy land was then drained and the land grazed; later on, the eighteenth century saw the beginnings of Ilkley as a spa centre. In 1756, a local squire built some moorside cottages known as White Wells to house the plunge baths where visitors could bathe and drink the very pure, but icy cold, water of a spring-fed moorland stream. To make the journey – often astride a donkey – from the town up to the baths more attractive, two lakes were enlarged. When a hydropathic centre was built at Ben Rhydding near Ilkley, this helped to make Ilkley a popular Victorian spa.

No doubt Victorian visitors would have made the effort to see some of the moor's spectacular rocky outcrops. These are made of millstone grit which closely resembles granite (indeed Charlotte Brontë mistook them for such). But, except for rocks brought down by glaciers, there are none of granitic origin in Yorkshire. Millstone grit outcrops, which feature throughout the Pennines, were formed by the deposition of sediments in a large shallow delta. Within these rocks are the fossil remains of tree-like giant club-mosses which flourished in the swamp forests during the Carboniferous Era 345 to 280 million years ago.

Since Victorian times, notable changes have taken place on the moor. Firstly, many of the gritstone rocks have been quarried and broken up for road-building, notably Bull Rock, the size of a cottage, which stood near the road beside the 'Cow and Calf' rocks. Secondly, the balance of plants which cover the moor has shifted. No longer is it possible to pick basketfuls of purple bilberries or, indeed, to see huge expanses of

purple heather-clad moor in late summer. In 1875 Ilkley Moor became a public pleasure ground, and as recently as the early part of this century, tourists were being lured to the moor by advertisements quoting it as 'a jewel set in heather'. Now, heather occurs only on the higher parts, as bracken has invaded the lower slopes and crowberry has increased so much it now dominates most of the moor.

This change, which has been a gradual, but continuous one, has been monitored by detailed vegetation surveys, which show there are several contributory factors. Being an urban common, grazing rights have been claimed by many Ilkley land owners, but it was not until the last World War that the numbers of sheep put out to graze began to change the make-up of the moor by their selective grazing. Not only do the sheep crop the heather close to the ground, but they also pull up the young plants. When the plants are allowed to flower they produce many tiny seeds which are dispersed by the wind and by animals accidentally brushing against the seed capsules. If the seeds land on bare peat they will germinate, but they can flourish only if there are few, if any, sheep in the area. Crowberry, on the other hand, has to depend on birds (notably grouse) and mammals to feed on its round black fruits and thereby disperse its seeds via their droppings, so that one plant does not produce such large numbers of seedlings as a single heather plant. However, it more than makes up for this by its rapid rate of shoot growth, increasing by as much as 30 centimetres (12 inches) a year.

In dry weather, moors are susceptible to accidental firing, and Ilkley Moor is no exception. The dry 1959 summer saw quite a few fires including some which burned deep into the peat and smouldered for weeks. Even ten years after this burn up, much of the ground was still barren, for the surface ash was eroded by wind and rain for a period of several years.

A local inhabitant of moorland, the spectacular emperor moth, here seen on gorse, spends its early life as a striking green and black caterpillar.

Several reservoirs fringing the moor that are fed by channels in its slopes also tend to dry up the soil. So, as a result of man's activities in recent years, Ilkley, like many other moors, is changing. Over a much longer time span, the climate also lends a hand in the shaping of the landscape. All our moorlands have been formed since the last Ice Age, when a prolonged period of wet weather encouraged the growth of the bog mosses. As the peat layers built up so shrubs and trees invaded the drier areas. Later on, when man wanted areas for grazing his stock, he began to clear away trees from the moors, and in post-war years parts of our wetter moorlands have been drained so that extensive areas of conifers can be planted. As farming and forestry spread over Britain's shrinking moorland, many attractive bogland plants, which cannot survive once the ground dries out, are fast disappearing.

BRITAIN'S LONGEST CANAL

The Leeds and Liverpool Canal is an awesome feat of engineering. The route of Britain's longest single canal takes it not only past the high-walled mills of industrial cities, but also through woodlands, fields and, most spectacular of all, across the Pennine moorlands. The 209-kilometre (127-mile) canal rises through 91 locks to a height of 148 metres (487 feet) above sea level and is fed by seven specially-built reservoirs.

Until the mid-eighteenth century, trading between Lancashire and Yorkshire was done entirely by pack-horse. Then John Longbottom, an imaginative engineer, persuaded Bradford businessmen and Liverpool merchants to back his plan to build a canal between the two counties, and in 1770 an authorising Act was passed. Work began at both ends of the canal, and long before the entire length was complete, local stretches at Leeds and Liverpool were opened for trading in 1774.

The most difficult part of the venture, constructing the canal across the Pennines, was finished in 1816, 46 years after work was first begun. This, in itself, is a record – the longest time taken for any of our canals to be built, and it was celebrated by great festivities, with a flotilla of boats sailing from Leeds to Liverpool. Two other canals were later constructed across the Pennines, but the Leeds and Liverpool is the only one which is still navigable.

In order to create a level route across undulating ground, canal engineers constructed the new waterways through cuttings and tunnels and over bridges and embankments. But where the land rose sharply, locks had to be built. On the steepest parts of the Leeds and Liverpool Canal, many of the locks are grouped close together, the most famous being the five rise 'staircase' at Bingley. Each lock leads directly into the neighbouring one through cliff-like gates, and the whole complex raises the water level 18 metres (60 feet) – a notable achievement of canal engineering. The original lock gates, which were made of English oak, lasted for 45–50 years.

The canal is noted for having over fifty swing bridges, twelve of which are 'roving bridges' built to carry the towpath, used by barge horses, from one side of the canal to the other. The towpath runs the entire length of the canal except through the two tunnels, one of which is nearly 1·5 kilometres (1 mile) long. Until the appearance of steam-tugs in the 1850s, professional leggers were used to move the boats along by lying down and pushing their feet against the tunnel walls and roof.

The canal was such a commercial success that for a long time it did not have to contend with competition from the railways. But in 1853 the Canal Company leased its trading revenues to railway companies who, by increasing the canal charges, effectively shifted traffic onto the railway lines. Despite this, the canal remained profitable until 1919 and the last cargo carried along it was a load of coal to Wigan power station in 1972.

Although the heyday of the canals fell between the mid-eighteenth and mid-nineteenth

The five-rise locks at Bingley form the steepest part of the Leeds-Liverpool Canal.

centuries, Britain's first canal – the Fossdyke Navigation – which crosses the Nottinghamshire and Lincolnshire border – was built by the Romans in the second century AD. By the end of the Industrial Revolution traffic had grown enormously and the canals provided a valuable arterial system for transporting freight from one part of the country to another. The 4,800 kilometres (3,000 miles) of routes were often constructed so that they linked up with navigable rivers.

These links were important to the development of canal wildlife. Aquatic plants and animals could migrate from one river system to another and the canals created a new habitat in which some river- and some pond-dwelling species could thrive alongside each other.

Seeding bulrushes and their reflections stand like sentinels at a canal's edge.

Slow-flowing canal water is generally unsuitable for plants and animals from highly oxygenated fast-flowing rivers, but it is ideal for floating plants which would get washed away in strong currents. On some canal stretches, duckweeds, and the very local water fern *Azolla*, which changes from green to pink in winter, completely carpet the water surface.

Countless freshwater springtails also live on the surface. They are so tiny that they resemble specks of soot, until viewed with a hand lens when their segmented wingless bodies can be seen. Pondskaters, water crickets and water measurers are all bugs which live on the water surface; the pondskaters are the most conspicuous, suddenly dashing across the surface film on their delicate legs. Whirligig beetles casually swim on the surface in a cluster, until a sudden movement either sends them whizzing round in tight circles or diving down beneath the surface.

In cross-section a canal is quite unlike a river, since the depth of the water beside each bank varies. Beside the towpath, the canal bank drops down steeply so that boats can tie up alongside, whereas usually the canal gradually shelves away from the offside bank. There are three distinct zones for wildlife in a canal, the

In a quiet backwater away from boat traffic, yellow water lilies can carpet the surface almost completely when their leaves are fully grown.

bank and towpath, which lead into the marginal shallows, which in turn give way to the deepest part, the central navigation channel.

As I strolled in July along the towpath of the Leeds and Liverpool Canal, between Bradford and Leeds, I found many bankside plants. Growing out of the brickwork built to strengthen part of an eroding bank were skullcap and gypsywort. At the muddy water's edge, clusters of water forget-me-not were struggling for space with meadowsweet intermingled with yellow

flags – long past their flowering prime and now bearing upright green fruits – clumps of bulrushes and outsized butterbur leaves. The graceful flowering rush was also there, with its umbels of pink flowers that are so attractive to hoverflies. Large bands of arrowhead were sending up erect spikes bearing white flowers in among the upright arrow-shaped leaves, one of the three different kinds produced by this plant. Those floating on the surface are oval, while underwater they are long and strap-shaped. Arrowhead produces special winter buds, called turions – each is bright blue with yellow spots – on the ends of runners. The turions sink down to the bottom where they remain over winter and each one gives rise to a new plant in the following spring. Frog-bit is another aquatic plant which produces winter turions, that float up to the surface in the spring.

Where the boat traffic is lightest, plants with large floating leaves such as yellow water lilies are able to thrive. After the flower has been pollinated by flies or bees, the distinctive bottle-shaped fruit develops, which gives the plant its alternative name of brandy bottle. When the ripe fruit splits the seeds are released inside a white fleshy mass which floats for several days before the seeds sink some distance downstream. Fish, coots, ducks and herons will eat these seeds and pass them out unharmed. Water lilies can also grow from fragments of their thick roots that are dredged up and dispersed when a canal is cleared.

From time to time, new plants and animals suddenly appear in canals. Sometimes these originate by aquarists dumping the entire contents of their tanks into the local canal. Some plants can be traced back to the seeds from plants in cotton and wool waste in mills on canal banks. Plants from warmer climes were able to flourish in warm water discharges from the mills, but as these closed down, the warm effluents ceased. When the canal temperature

dropped, these alien plants were no longer able to flower and produce seeds. However, those which are able to grow simply from tiny fragments, without producing seeds can spread very rapidly through a whole canal system.

Canadian pondweed is one such plant which was introduced to Ireland in 1836 and is now recorded over most of lowland Britain in canals, rivers and ponds.

The zebra mussel is a stripy bivalve mollusc of brackish and fresh water. It appeared in Britain in 1824 and was probably introduced on the bottom of ships sailing from the Baltic. Moving into our canal system via estuaries and rivers, by 1840 it had spread over much of Britain, accelerated by its planktonic larvae which drift in the water currents.

Like ponds, once canals fall into disuse, they gradually silt up as decaying reeds slow down the water flow. Eventually they become completely choked with aquatic plants and ultimately brambles, willows and alders move in. By this stage, the animal life associated with the open water has gone, and the canal becomes a marshy tangle of shrubs.

When there is some open water, animal life is abundant. Among the most numerous canal dwellers are the water fleas and copepods which feed on microscopic plants and are themselves preyed upon by hydra. This freshwater relation of sea anemones lives attached to water plants and the undersides of fallen leaves, grabbing at unsuspecting water fleas which brush against its outstretched tentacles. In summer, canal water abounds with other invertebrate animals. There are worms, water snails, water beetles, water boatmen, freshwater shrimps and water lice, as well as the larval stage of insects such as dragonflies, mayflies,

Damselflies hold their curious mating position for a number of hours before the female breaks away to lay her eggs in the water.

In the overgrown shallows of a little-used canal, a toad noses its way to the water's surface to breathe among the duckweed.

stoneflies and caddisflies which emerge from the water as adults.

Fish have moved into canals by swimming in from connecting rivers and by anglers introducing them, so that some canals now harbour a good variety of species. Among the most widespread are sticklebacks, minnows, roach, tench, bream, perch, pike and carp. Little evidence of these will be seen from a walk along the towpath, although the white lacy ropes of perch spawn laid in April can be quite conspicuous when the water level is low.

Amphibians often use canals as breeding sites, especially where there are weed-choked shallows. Each year, I keep a check on the frogs and toads that return to breed in a local stretch of the Basingstoke Canal. In mild years all the frogs are gone before the first toad appears, but when spring comes late, their breeding period overlaps, although the toads seek deeper water for spawning than the frogs.

Although commercial canal traffic has now virtually ceased, pleasure boat traffic has increased dramatically in recent years, and many abandoned stretches have been renovated. However, on the Leeds and Liverpool Canal, pleasure boats are not particularly common, since it takes a lot of hard work to get a boat up through the locks to the most scenic central section. This is good for the canal's wildlife since plants of the water's edge get destroyed at mooring sites and also by the wash created by fast boats. Boat propellers also tear off fragments of submerged plants, and the repeated stirring up of the mud makes the water more turbid. This reduces the amount of light reaching the underwater plants, slowing down the plant growth on which most canal animals ultimately rely.

Surveys of the breeding birds carried out on an overgrown stretch and a well used part of the Leeds and Liverpool Canal show that a rich assortment of plants attracts a much wider range of resident water and terrestrial birds. Along a 3-kilometre (2-mile) overgrown stretch, 82 pairs of birds of 17 different species were found breeding. These included 17 pairs of moorhens, 10 pairs of coots, 8 pairs of mallards, 1 pair each of mute swans and little grebes, 16 pairs of sedge warblers, and 9 pairs of reed buntings. When this was compared with a part regularly kept clear by dredging and herbicides, only 26 nesting pairs and 4 species were recorded in a stretch of almost twice the length. This convincingly shows that the canals with little boating are much richer habitats for wetland wildlife. I can well recall a stretch of the Shropshire Union Canal leading into a boating marina, which has a poor selection of plants on the banks and in the water. Adjacent to this, in the other direction is a reserve area where the bankside plants are so lush that they make an almost impenetrable barrier between the towpath and the water.

Canals are also used for many other leisure pursuits which affect their water and their banks. Some stretches may be set aside for canoeing or rowing, while towpaths which are not too overgrown are used for cycling, horse-riding and angling.

But canals are not only useful as pleasure grounds. They provide easily accessible sites for enjoying and studying freshwater life. Many already have nature trails along short stretches and now that more and more derelict canals are being renovated the network of waterways contested by boaters and conservationists looks set to increase.

LIVING WALLS

The old city of York is enclosed by one of the most complete medieval city walls still standing in England. From whichever direction you approach the city, you inevitably meet the overpowering walls built high on earth ramparts, towering above the road level. The Romans built a fortress here in 71 AD which was bordered by an open ditch backed by an earthen bank and a wooden palisade. The fortress was later strengthened in the fourth century when the wooden palisade was replaced by a 6-metre (21-foot) high stone wall. After the Romans departed in 410 AD, the original walls were no longer maintained and they gradually began to decay and crumble.

Over the centuries, various measures were taken to improve the defences of the city. In the ninth and eleventh centuries, the earth ramparts were raised by the Danes and the Normans and at a later stage a moat was added so the walls could be penetrated only across a drawbridge sited at each gateway. The present walls which stretch for over 3 kilometres (2 miles) round the old city were built in the thirteenth and fourteenth centuries of magnesian limestone blocks quarried from Tadcaster. The cost of building and maintaining the walls was met by 'murage' taxes – tolls levied on goods brought into the city. Each year four Muremasters were elected, who were responsible for making sure that the walls were well maintained.

Oxford ragwort, growing out between the blocks of stone, brings a splash of colour to part of the old walls in the city of York.

Throughout the time the walls were the major defence of the city, they were never allowed to fall into a state of disrepair, but by the latter part of the eighteenth century, they had been abandoned and had begun to decay, so that by the onset of the nineteenth century, the City Council decided that they would have to be renewed for safety reasons. Then in 1827, the York Footpath Association was formed and through their action the walls were saved. After extensive repairs and rebuilding had been carried out, the final section of the Wall Walk was opened in 1889. The walls, the four major gates or Bars, and the thirty-seven towers, became scheduled as Ancient Monuments in 1922 and they are now maintained by an Inspector of Ancient Monuments who supervises eight stonemasons, with one apprentice and one labourer.

Anyone who has time to wander through York will inevitably be tempted to walk the walls, for there are some splendid views from these unique walkways from where you can piece together much of the city's ancient history. As well as appreciating the views, I was also intrigued to see what evidence I could find of wildlife on this huge circle of masonry. Many plants had gained a foothold – from minute seedlings to large trees – but traces of animals were much harder to find. Repeated daily trampling prevents most plants from establishing themselves on the actual walkway. This becomes immediately apparent when a stretch which is under repair, and therefore closed to the public, is compared with an open stretch. Within a few months, a closed section will begin

Such a profuse growth of moss and lichen on a wall may take many years to develop.

to sprout a colourful array of wild flowers such as yellow coltsfoot, hawkbit and purple rosebay willowherb.

A glance at the walls in any town will show just how varied these man-made structures are.

Their location, whether in shade or sun, their aspect – north, south, east or west, the structure and the acidity or alkalinity of their building blocks, and the method used to bond them together are all factors which will affect the rate at which plants invade them. Walls which retain moisture are more likely to harbour mosses and ferns than dry walls, whereas lichens will thrive on the tops of the latter, providing that the surrounding air is not polluted with sulphur dioxide. Limestone walls are, of course, most likely to be colonised by lime-loving plants, even in areas well away from natural limestone. Weathering of the rock also influences the rate that plants establish themselves, since pits or hollows in the rock will trap nutritious humus and dust which would otherwise blow off. In recent years, 'acid rain', formed when the gas sulphur dioxide dissolves in rain water, is helping to accelerate the weathering of walls, since it attacks the mortared joints and even the walling itself if it is made of limestone. In Europe alone, some 30 million tonnes of sulphur dioxide are released into the atmosphere each year.

Apart from dry stone walls, which are constructed by carefully positioning each individual stone one upon another, walls are made by bonding stones or bricks together using mortar. Right up until the end of the last century, brick and stone walls were bonded with a soft calcareous mortar. This was made from a mixture of lime, sand, loam, straw and, surprisingly, cattle dung. This mortar was not at all durable and soon crumbled away, creating cracks and crevices in which humus accumulated, so that microscopic algae could grow, paving the way for mosses, and later for flowering plants to take root. Once pioneer plants have established themselves they cast shade and trap moisture for other plants and provide shelter and food for small invertebrate animals. Although they are rarely seen, these

As mortar crumbles away between the brickwork so cracks appear allowing plants such as this red dead nettle to take root.

animals – springtails, nematodes and tardi-grades – can be very numerous and they are able to survive prolonged periods of drought. Woodlice, centipedes, snails, spiders and bee-tles also frequent wall crevices and help to feed shrews, voles and birds. Wrens will nest in old walls, as will robins and blackbirds if a large hole appears after a brick drops out. Walls beside streams provide nesting sites for grey wagtails and dippers, while wheatears make use of the drystone walls of hill country districts. However cement rather than mortar is now used to bond bricks or stones together. This is so hard that it takes much longer to weather; and these walls tend to harbour a much poorer selection of plants than mortar-bonded walls.

Since soil naturally accumulates and rain water collects at the base of walls, these parts generally support many more plants than the wall tops. However, in places with a high rainfall where the atmosphere tends to be humid, mosses will colonise the top of a wall only a year or two after it has been erected. Ants and birds both help to make walls more fertile for plants; ants by carrying soil into cracks and crevices, and birds by depositing their nitrogen-rich droppings.

Clues to the plants which regularly inhabit walls can often be gleaned from their common names: the fern – wall rue spleenwort – and the wild flowers – wall lettuce, wall pepper, wall pennywort, pellitory-of-the-wall, wallflower, stony-in-the-wall (a Lincolnshire name for shepherd's purse) and wallwort (a Shropshire name for danewort).

It is not difficult to imagine how plants appeared at the base of a wall, but it is interesting to speculate how they began their life on, or near, the top of a vertical wall. Plants with hairy seeds or fruits, such as dandelion, hawkbit and Oxford ragwort (see page 60) can climb to the top of a wall as their hairy fruits are buoyed up in the slightest of breezes and slowly parachuted downwards. Woody nightshade, yew and alder all produce attractive fruits which are dispersed by birds either accidentally dropping them as they gorge themselves, or passing them out as seeds in their droppings as they perch on top of a wall. Yellow corydalis is a plant with seeds which are far too heavy – each one weighs one-hundredth of a gramme (three-thousandths of an ounce) – to be carried any distance by wind, yet more often than not, this attractive introduced plant grows near the tops of walls. It gets there by ants carrying the black shiny seeds into crevices. Each seed bears a nutritious part rich in oil, known as an elaio-some, which is highly attractive to ants. Wallflower and greater celandine are other wall plants which also produce ant-attracting seeds with elaiosomes.

Ivy-leaved toadflax, which was introduced to Britain in 1640, now covers walls all over the country. It is a plant which is extremely well adapted to a wall life. The fleshy leaves, like those of stonecrop and wall pennywort, are well able to withstand drought, but it is the changing response of the plant to light which is most remarkable. Initially, the stalks of the leaves and flowers grow towards the light, but after the flowers have been pollinated, the stalks grow longer and shun light, growing instead towards the darker wall crevices where the seed capsules split, scattering the seeds in a suitable place for germination to occur rather than into the air.

There are other wall plants, such as pellitory-of-the-wall, which have no obvious device for getting their seeds lodged high up walls. The only explanation for their success at this seems to be that they drop their seeds or fruits from the top of the plant and when these grow, they in their turn, will continue the upward trend. Man, too, unwittingly plays his part in dispersing seeds. As he walks around seeds are pressed into mud on the soles of his shoes or fall into his trouser turn-ups when they happen to be in fashion. Out of curiosity one botanist grew several hundred plants from seeds collected in his turn-ups!

In general, plants which grow on walls are opportunists, quick to make use of a chance to spread, like all plants of waste ground. As I climbed a flight of steps from the road onto the York Walls, I noticed a patch of seedlings sprouting among the rotting leaves, cigarette stubs and sweet papers which had collected in the corners where the steps butted up against the wall. I knew that these seedlings would have little chance of establishing themselves once they had been spotted by tidy-minded city road sweepers. Beneath a seat I noticed sycamore seedlings growing in regimental lines between the stone blocks. These progeny of an overhanging sycamore tree may have survived human trampling, but they would not be allowed to reach any substantial size, since it has been decided recently that no trees will, in future, be planted on the ramparts or be sited within 10 metres (33 feet) of the wall fence, to prevent damage to the monument by the roots.

It was with some surprise that I found an isolated clump of liverworts flourishing at the base of the vertical wall, since these delicate non-flowering plants survive only in damp places. Presumably, the rain water which drained off the walls was channelled into the spot where liverwort spores happened to alight. Although liverworts, like mosses and ferns, do

Once established on a wall, ivy-leaved toadflax soon spreads by scattering its seed into the cracks between the interlocking stones.

not produce colourful showy flowers, they are well worth a closer look with a magnifying lens for their intricate shapes. It was the miniature green parasols of the common liverwort which caught my eye as I strolled along the York Walls. These parasols bear the male reproductive organs, while the female ones are borne on star-like structures on separate plants. The name liverwort is derived from the practice in the days of early medicine of naming plants after any resemblance they might have to a human organ, and indeed some liverworts do vaguely resemble lobes of the liver.

A small group of related species of spiders, called *Segestria*, are almost confined to walls, although they do also live beneath stones and bark. They build an elaborate wall web, comprising a silken tunnel penetrating a wall crevice and, radiating out from the tunnel entrance, a dozen thick threads which act as 'fishing lines'. The spider sits inside the tunnel with its legs resting on these 'lines'. When an unsuspecting insect alights on any one of the threads, the spider immediately dashes out and seizes its prey — a response which can be induced by carefully touching one of the threads with a vibrating tuning fork.

In the autumn, snails, queen wasps, small tortoiseshell and peacock butterflies have to seek a dry place in which to spend the winter and so they often use crevices in walls as their hideouts.

Although new walls are still being built today, both brick and stone are now costly raw materials and this, coupled with the greatly increased cost of labour, means that we are unlikely to see a modern replica of an engineering achievement comparable with the York Walls. Gradually, cheaper modern substitutes for older walling materials are beginning to appear in our towns, most notably as vast areas of concrete. The highly durable and usually smooth surface of concrete does not encourage plant growth which tends to accentuate the walls' starkness. We must thank past generations of wall-makers for adding so much interest and colour to the city landscape.

A WOOD
PREPARES FOR WINTER

Britain's deciduous woods are at their best twice a year, in May and October. May heralds spring with fresh green leaves and carpets of flowers, while October marks the end of the trees' growing season with a riot of autumnal colours, and with toadstools which seem to appear almost overnight.

Strid Woods, which border both sides of the River Wharfe on the Bolton Abbey Estate, convey the very essence of autumn when the leaves of the trees are on the turn. On the woodland floor, decaying stumps are then an attractive mix of colours – the darker wood setting off the yellow or gold fallen leaves, the green mosses and a clump or two of toadstools. Together they blend into a harmonious design, creating a miniature garden sprouting from the rotting wood. Since the toadstools soon collapse and die after they appear, these tiny gardens are at their prime for only a few brief days each year.

We have to thank the Reverend William Carr – the incumbent of Bolton Priory Church from 1789 to 1843 – for laying out the paths in Strid Woods in the early part of the nineteenth century. In those days, visitors were few and far between, but once the railway came to Bolton Abbey in 1888 it brought the picturesque woods and the spectacular views of the River Wharfe within easy reach of inhabitants of the nearby industrial towns.

One path by the river leads to the Strid, the feature that gave the woods their name. Here, the river waters are channelled into such a narrow rocky chasm that, in theory, a person can stride across it. However, the moss-covered rocks are so slippery that it would be foolhardy to attempt such a crossing; indeed, more than one life has been lost in this way. The Strid was formed when a series of pot-holes joined up to form a chasm, and an underwater survey carried out in 1974 by sub-aqua divers revealed that the rocks on either side of the Strid have been undercut by the racing waters.

The mix of trees, which gives the woods such a variety of colour in autumn, is made up of some large specimen oak, beech, sycamore and ash trees, which were planted some 250 to 300 years ago. Some of the older broadleaved trees have been felled, while others have decayed through old age but, over the years, more hardwoods have been planted to replace them. Faster-growing conifers, including Scots pine, larch and Douglas fir have also been planted.

Except in the mildest parts of Britain, few, if any, of the woodland flowers linger on until autumn, for the passing of the autumn equinox on September 21st inevitably heralds showers and gales, as well as colder nights. Then, in most woods, the plants which are still flowering can be counted on one hand. In Strid Woods, I did notice herb Robert scrambling over a dead tree trunk with some pink flowers as late as the end of September, but at this time of year toadstools or fungi are in their prime.

For a few brief days each autumn, the beech trees in Strid Woods are a cascade of colour.

After the ground has had a good soaking and the days are still warm, it is well worth exploring old woodlands where there are plenty of tree stumps, rotting leaves and humus on which fungi live. For most of the year, fungi grow beneath the ground or in wood producing a network of branching strands called a mycelium which penetrates the food source. The part which we see above the ground – the toadstool – produces the spores which disperse the fungus to other sites.

Some fungi can spell death even to healthy trees. No forester or gardener welcomes the parasitic honey fungus, for example, which attacks a wide variety of living trees – mostly hardwoods. The toadstools of this fungus sprout from a network of thick black branches – known as 'boot laces' – running beneath the bark of the infected tree, and appear in dense clusters of several dozen or more at the base of the trunk. The top or cap of each one is at first yellowish, but as it enlarges and flattens out it turns brown. Sometimes these fungi are coated with a fine white dust of microscopic spores which are shed in dry weather from the gills beneath the cap.

As well as many clumps of honey fungus in Strid Woods, I found the delicate sulphur tuft, which grows in large clusters on dead wood and has much smaller bright yellow caps. Candle snuff fungus also grows on dead wood, and may be found throughout the year. Once seen, the diminutive black antlers with white tips are quite distinctive.

I detected one fungus – the stinkhorn – by its powerful odour long before I actually saw it. Aptly named from its powerful aroma of rotting flesh, stinkhorns grow almost anywhere – including gardens. Each one starts life as an underground spherical 'egg' which, once it breaks the ground, grows almost visibly. Once the hollow white stalk is formed, the cells in its outer spongy wall simply enlarge within a matter of hours. The top of the stinkhorn is covered with a greenish slimy mass of spores and it is this which produces the stench to attract flies. Depending on the number of stinkhorns in a wood, a single fungus may be completely covered with flies of all sizes and colours. As they feed, spores adhere to their feet and get dispersed around the woodland.

Puffballs, and the related earth stars, have an intriguing method of dispersing their spores which are contained inside a thin-walled sac. When the spores are ripe, the sac splits on top and any pressure on it – from rain drops to an inquisitive mouse – squeezes out some microscopic spores like a puff of smoke. The spores can be very numerous – a single giant puffball produces many million. They are so light that they easily get wafted up into air currents like seeds of flowering plants. Many will land in unsuitable places, but some will end up where they can ultimately grow into new toadstools. In Strid Woods, I noticed fungi were sprouting where their spores had lodged on the wooden litter containers and even in the corner of the birdwatchers' hide!

In some southern woods, notably beech-woods in Dorset, Wiltshire, Hampshire, Sussex and Kent, edible fungi known as truffles were gathered using special truffle-hunting dogs which could scent a truffle from over 30 metres (35 yards) away. Sometimes this delectable underground fungus was also found by lying prone on the ground so that swarms of truffle flies hovering just above the truffle could be spotted. The Wiltshire village of Winterslow was a renowned centre for professional truffle hunters, and it was here that this unusual means of earning a livelihood ceased in Britain in 1935. Truffles are, however, still gathered with great secrecy in woods in parts of France.

The fluted brackets of the sulphur polypore fungus are proof that the heart of this tree is already rotting away.

At the start of the pannage season, pigs in the New Forest are allowed to run free to forage for the acorns produced by the ancient oaks.

When sun shines on a mature broadleaved tree in full leaf a great deal of water is lost by evaporation through the leaves. For example, a birch tree can lose as much as 60–70 litres (13–15 gallons) in a day, and some 60 per cent of the annual rain falling on a large beech wood gets recycled into the atmosphere within this period. If this loss is not replaced by the roots taking up more water from the soil, the trees would soon begin to wilt. In many parts of Strid Woods ramifying tree roots are visible where the overlying soil has been washed away. But these are not the roots which draw up the water – it is the tiny rootlets which do this job. If the ground is frozen, the roots are unable to draw up water, so deciduous trees shed their leaves in autumn as an insurance against water loss during winter.

Before the leaves are shed, however, they turn colour. The intensity varies not only from one species to another but also among individual trees. In autumn when the daylight hours decrease, the production of chlorophyll, which gives the leaves their green colour, stops, and the other leaf pigments – previously masked – begin to show through. Sycamore and Norway maple leaves turn bright yellow, while beech leaves turn orangey-brown, and guelder rose a rich red. Warm autumn days interspersed with cold nights produce the best colours, although the leaves themselves can vanish overnight in a raging storm.

The larch, one of the few deciduous conifers grown in Britain, also turns an attractive golden shade in autumn, while Scots pine, yew, spruces and firs are evergreen conifers which shed their leaves – a few at a time – throughout the year. The leaves of these trees, the narrow 'needles', have a thick outer skin and a small number of pores through which water is lost. They survive the winter by conserving what little water is available. Pine needles also roll inwards along their length.

While birds feast on autumnal fruits, squirrels, jays and mice gather up nuts and berries to stock their winter larders. As these animals collect up heavy fruits, such as acorns and beech nuts, they drop a few, helping to disperse them through the woods. If ideal weather conditions prevail in May for the oak and beech flowers to be successfully wind-pollinated, acorns and beech nuts will be produced in the following autumn in vast numbers. When bumper crops of beech nuts, or 'mast', are formed, the weight of the massed fruits can be so great that heavily laden branches break off the trees.

The Domesday Book records swine rents – the number of pigs which tenants paid each year in return for the right to fatten them on acorns. One of the five Rights of Common of the New Forest still allows commoners to put their pigs out in the Forest during the Pannage Season. This is a period of not less than 60 consecutive days during the autumn when the acorns and beech-mast have fallen. The Forest of Dean is another ancient forest where pannage rights still apply today.

Once the leaves have fallen, the shape of the trees, as well as the colour and texture of their barks, can be appreciated and compared. The smooth straight beech trunks contrast with the furrowed oaks or the scaly sycamores, and in ancient forests the unnatural bizarre shapes of pollarded trees are especially eerie when shrouded in autumnal mists.

Where the rainfall is high and the air clean, lichens can encrust old trees so completely that little of the natural bark is visible. It is in these lichen curtains and bark crevices that many insects seek their winter hideouts. Moths and butterflies may overwinter in any one of the four

stages of their life-cycle – the egg, the caterpillar, the chrysalis or pupa, and the adult. While searching for woodland fungi in autumn, I have often seen a hairy caterpillar of the pale tussock moth crawling over fallen leaves in search of a place to pupate before the onset of winter.

Crotches of old trees can provide cosy winter quarters for small mammals – providing water does not accumulate in the base, while hollow trees provide roosts for bats. Up in the central forks of trees, grey squirrels build their winter homes or dreys – distinct from their summer dreys which are built out on the branches away from the trunk.

Winter is a time when animals and plants both need to conserve their water supplies and energy. Annual plants die down completely and survive as seeds or fruits, while perennials die down to ground level but overwinter as underground tubers. Once trees have shed their leaves, the overwintering buds remain dormant until the following spring. Before the dormouse hibernates in its winter nest it lays in food, just in case it happens to wake up. Birds have to forage throughout winter and when the ground is frozen they have to work hard to glean what they can. The urge to feed is so great that in severe winters timid birds will emerge from the safety of their cover and tolerate an exceptionally close approach. Their chorus of song will not begin until the days begin to lengthen; before then the winter woodland is a quiet and peaceful place in which to contemplate the past year and to look forward to the next.

A rich autumnal mosaic of sulphur tuft fungi, mosses and fallen beech leaves.

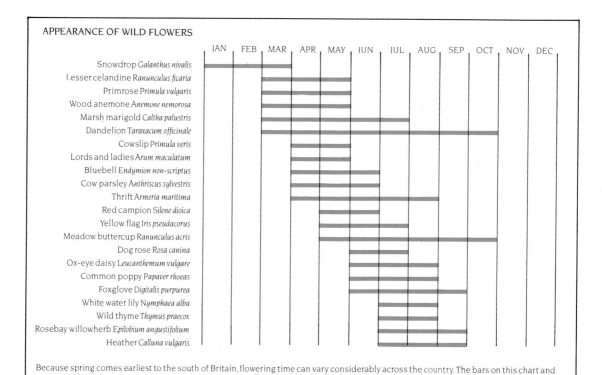

APPEARANCE OF WILD FLOWERS

	JAN	FEB	MAR	APR	MAY	JUN	JUL	AUG	SEP	OCT	NOV	DEC

Snowdrop *Galanthus nivalis*
Lesser celandine *Ranunculus ficaria*
Primrose *Primula vulgaris*
Wood anemone *Anemone nemorosa*
Marsh marigold *Caltha palustris*
Dandelion *Taraxacum officinale*
Cowslip *Primula veris*
Lords and ladies *Arum maculatum*
Bluebell *Endymion non-scriptus*
Cow parsley *Anthriscus sylvestris*
Thrift *Armeria maritima*
Red campion *Silene dioica*
Yellow flag *Iris pseudacorus*
Meadow buttercup *Ranunculus acris*
Dog rose *Rosa canina*
Ox-eye daisy *Leucanthemum vulgare*
Common poppy *Papaver rhoeas*
Foxglove *Digitalis purpurea*
White water lily *Nymphaea alba*
Wild thyme *Thymus praecox*
Rosebay willowherb *Epilobium angustifolium*
Heather *Calluna vulgaris*

Because spring comes earliest to the south of Britain, flowering time can vary considerably across the country. The bars on this chart and on the one for trees (*below*) show the complete flowering period throughout Britain for each species.

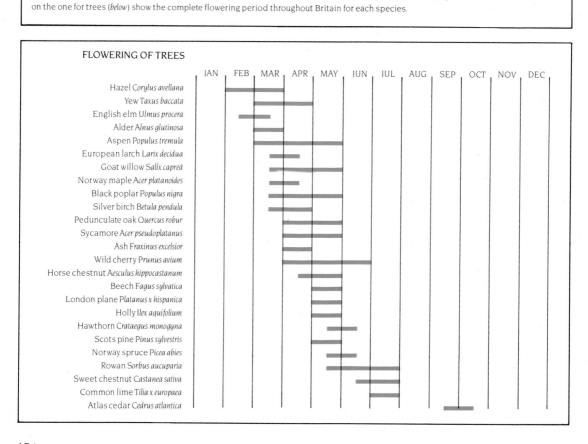

FLOWERING OF TREES

	JAN	FEB	MAR	APR	MAY	JUN	JUL	AUG	SEP	OCT	NOV	DEC

Hazel *Corylus avellana*
Yew *Taxus baccata*
English elm *Ulmus procera*
Alder *Alnus glutinosa*
Aspen *Populus tremula*
European larch *Larix decidua*
Goat willow *Salix caprea*
Norway maple *Acer platanoides*
Black poplar *Populus nigra*
Silver birch *Betula pendula*
Pedunculate oak *Quercus robur*
Sycamore *Acer pseudoplatanus*
Ash *Fraxinus excelsior*
Wild cherry *Prunus avium*
Horse chestnut *Aesculus hippocastanum*
Beech *Fagus sylvatica*
London plane *Platanus x hispanica*
Holly *Ilex aquifolium*
Hawthorn *Crataegus monogyna*
Scots pine *Pinus sylvestris*
Norway spruce *Picea abies*
Rowan *Sorbus aucuparia*
Sweet chestnut *Castanea sativa*
Common lime *Tilia x europaea*
Atlas cedar *Cedrus atlantica*

APPEARANCE OF BUTTERFLIES

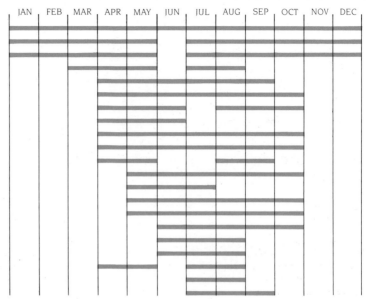

This chart shows when the adults of our commonest species may be seen. The timing of butterfly life cycles is varied. Some overwinter as adults and emerge on the first warm spring day, whereas others overwinter as eggs, caterpillars or chrysalids, and their adults emerge only in summer. Some species produce as many as four generations in a year.

INDEX